When The Laughter Dies:

A True Account Of A Firefighter/EMT

And His Struggles With PTSD

Paul D. Barnes, Sr.

Dedicated to...

My dad, for driving me all those times.

My children.

Table of Contents:

Introduction

In 37 years, you tend to see some horrific shit. I've seen things most people only see in movies. I've seen just about every imaginable punishment the human body can take: men, women, children. I have fallen through a roof at a fire, I've had to jump from a second story window at a fire. And with no outlets —here comes PTSD.

The old timers used to tell us, "You have to laugh it off. If you don't, it'll eat you alive." I guess I didn't laugh hard enough.

The Early Years

When I was young, we would go visit my grandparents in West Haven. I can remember my grandfather taking me to the fire station to see the fire trucks. I remember seeing the fire pole. I wanted to slide down that pole so badly. They wouldn't let me because I was too young. I couldn't tell you who came with us. I just know my grandfather took me there. I think I kind of knew then that I wanted to be a firefighter.

I would bounce back and forth between wanting to be a cop and wanting to be a firefighter, especially having a state trooper for a father. But I think the thing that did it for me was the TV show *Emergency*. I can remember pretending that I was either Johnny Gage or Roy DeSoto. Pretending I was a firefighter/paramedic was just the coolest thing ever.

And then, one day, my oldest brother and I were going across town on an errand for my mom. The local fire chief flew past us, lights and siren. My brother followed him. We arrived at a fully involved house fire before any fire trucks got there.

I just remember him telling me, "Stay in the car!"

He ran up to the house. It seemed like forever until he came back. He was soaking wet, and smelled of smoke. My brother told me he'd been running around the outside of the house, making sure no one was inside. I remember the firefighters pulling up then; the guys getting out of the trucks in their full turnout gear and pulling the hoses off. I knew what I wanted. It wasn't so much what I wanted, it was what I had to do.

Because of that day, my oldest brother and my other brother both joined the local fire department. They would take me with them when they went to the fire house. I counted the days until I turned sixteen. That's when I could ride the trucks. I truly had no idea what I was in for.

In May of 1978, I turned sixteen. I had my membership application filled out and on the chief's desk in record time.

In June of '78, I was voted in as an active member. That meeting was the most important meeting to me. Unfortunately, it as the same night as my grandmother's testimonial dinner. (The Veteran's Hospital gave her a dinner honoring her for many, many years of volunteering.) I love my grandmother, but I was not a happy camper. The next day, my dad drove me to the fire chief's place of business, which happened to be across the street from the fire station. I was promptly sworn in as a member of the fire department. The chief then handed me my very own plastic key card, to get me into the fire station. He told me to go across the street and find a pair of boots, a coat and a helmet that would fit me.

Back in the late seventies, turnout gear consisted of hip boots (rubber fire boots which would either pull up to your hip or fold down), a long coat (made of rubber or a new material, Nomex), and a plastic helmet. My gloves were rubber. I don't think my feet touched the ground from his front door to the fire house front door. In record time, I had my own boots, my own coat and my own helmet. I think if I could have slept in them that night, I probably would have.

The Rookie Years

At the time of writing this, I am 52 years old. Things that happened when I was 18 might be out of sequence, but they're still worthy of mention.

I remember the first house fire I went to. It was a neighbor and family friend. It was around Christmas time. I crawled on my hands and knees through the house, passing by the Christmas tree and the presents, and hoping the family could still open their gifts.

Back then, we had two air packs on Engine 1 and two air packs on Engine 2. If you weren't one of the first ones there, you didn't get one. One of the old timers grabbed me off the hose line and told me to put an air pack on before I went in. That was the first fire that I ever fought as a firefighter. I don't think I slept that night, I was on such a high. My enthusiasm was based on the fact that we were able to put the fire out and minimize the damage. The home-owners were extremely grateful. The guy was making drinks at his bar in the basement of his minimally-burned house, thanks to the efforts of the energetic volunteers that we were.

There was one call where I learned really quickly that I needed to be educated. It was night time, so it was dark. We received a call for smoke in the basement. I had my turnout gear with me at home. My dad drove me to the call (it was on the next street down from us), and I met the homeowner in the driveway. She said that the clothes in her dryer had caught fire and she believed it was out. I put my turnout gear on, went into the smoke-filled basement with no air pack, located the dryer and opened it. I found smoldering clothes, consisting of t-shirts, briefs and socks. I put on my gloves, figuring I'm going to eradicate the problem and save the day. I scooped the clothes up in my arms and walked out the door. As soon as the clothes hit the open air, they burst into flames. I threw them down into the driveway.

I laughed to myself, *Wow, I dodged a bullet on that one! I could of burned myself really badly!* I marched back into the basement, got the remaining clothes out of the dryer, and holding them out in front of me, I walked outside. These didn't so much didn't burst into flames—they smoked a lot and then caught fire. I put them down in the driveway. That was the last of the clothes from the dryer.

I went back into the house, opening some windows to ventilate the smoke. I explained to the arriving fire chief that the problem had been removed from the house and that I had done it. He proceeded to counsel me on entering a building, first of all, without proper training and without proper equipment. Then he told me that I did a good job. When the situation was contained, we were cleared to leave. I went back home, feeling very proud of myself and my accomplishments. Until I woke up the next morning with cyanide poisoning.

Cyanide poisoning was the byproduct of the cotton and polyester clothes burning. My eyes swelled up and shut, I couldn't see. My face blew up like a balloon. It was then I figured I'd better start going to fire school. I did nothing different than any other enthusiastic, energetic, over-zealous sixteen-year-old, that was new to the fire department, would do. They don't know any better. I didn't know any better.

The Start Of Paul Barnes, Firefighter

Soon after joining the department, I was given some training on the basics: hoses, tools and operations. What to do, what not to do and what was expected of me. I wanted to learn as much as I could. I had waited for this moment for so long. Then someone told me about fire school. I was in.

Our fire school was located in Willimantic, CT. It consisted of two buildings housing classrooms, a building where the cafeteria was located, a two-story building used for simulating building fires but was also used in rescue scenarios and an area known as "the pits". These were three separate concrete trenches filled with water and used oil that was lit on fire. Crews learned how to attack fires involving petroleum products. There was also an area for LPG (liquefied petroleum gas) or propane fires. There was a large propane tank prop that we used for LPG fires and a prop called "the Christmas tree" which was just a straight vertical pipe with many other pipes coming off of it. This was lit so we could learn to fight propane fires.

Prior to the 1980's, all firefighting training was broken down into blocks. There was basic firefighting, which was the beginning. We learned about hoses: how to load them on the apparatus, how to carry them, how to use them and on which fires to use which size. We also were taught proper hose streams for fighting certain fires. This is where I first learned about crawling low under smoke, search and rescue, and ladder operations. We utilized the burn building for our search and rescue, hose advancement and ventilation. It wasn't until we got to the pits that we actually got to fight real fire. I can't begin to explain the exhilaration I felt the first time I held a charged hose line and advanced it toward real fire. The feeling of accomplishment when the fire went out was mind blowing for me. That was it, I was hooked.

Most classes were held on the weekends so it was easy for me to attend. The fire department I belonged to paid for us to attend these classes and, on most occasions, the fire chief bought us lunch. I was never denied any classes and we always had a crew of members who attended. At the completion of each training class we were given certificates for our accomplishments. The fire department required a copy of all certificates I earned to be placed into my permanent training file.

Other classes I attended were: Vehicle Rescue, where I learned how to gain access to people who were trapped in vehicles as a result of an accident. I was trained on the use of the Jaws of Life, a Porta-Power, which was a portable hydraulic spreader just like the Jaws, only manually operated by hand and not a gas-powered pump. I was taught to use pry bars, crowbars and chains, all of which had their own uses for extrication. I was basically taught how to dismantle a vehicle (any vehicle) and remove an injured person without doing them more harm. That was cool.

Pretty soon my folder in the station was filling up with

certificates, as well as the shoe box I had at home. I was proud of my accomplishments so far. Here I was, 16 years old and a certified firefighter. I felt like I could take on anything that was thrown at me. I didn't feel like I knew it all, but I was willing to try and I had a good start at it. Any time a class was held at the fire school, I wanted to attend. Pretty soon, a class on car fires was offered. I went to the chief with my application for the class in hand, placed it on his desk and asked for him to approve it. As with the other classes, he signed it and asked what I wanted for lunch. He took really good care of his people. My other classes would come much later on, but for right now, I was on top of the world. I went from pretending to be a fireman as a kid to being a certified firefighter at the age of 16. I wanted something more, though. The department I was in also ran an ambulance. That was it, I wanted to be medically trained.

Medically Trained

The first medical training I had was Advanced First Aid given by the American Heart Association. The classes were held at my high school at night in three hour blocks. The classes ran for 4 or 5 weeks and I learned about bleeding control, splinting, burns and exposure to caustic chemicals and how to treat them. We practiced on each other in class, splinting imaginary broken bones and bandaging cuts. At the end there was a written test. When I passed, I received a certificate and a card to carry in my wallet. Now I was able to help at medical calls and car accidents.

I won't lie, I was scared when I went to my first medical call. I was afraid I'd do something wrong or not do enough to help. My AFA certification was very limited on what I could do, so there were not many calls I could help on.

Then the State of Connecticut started a MRT program. Medical Response Technician was a step above Advanced First Aid and a step below Emergency Medical Technician. I thought, I need to do this. I asked the fire chief to sign me up.

My MRT classes were held at a neighboring fire department. Myself and one other person from my department attended. This class was much more in depth. Not only did we learn how to bandage and splint, now we were being taught CPR, how to recognize heart attacks and stroke, treating bee stings and assisting in applying backboards. Classes were four hours a night, twice a week ,and went on for about 3 months. Everything was much more detailed and explained more thoroughly. The CPR portion of the class was a separate certification. I took a separate written exam for that and had to do a practical demonstration of my skills. Once that was done, I received a CPR certification card to carry with me. I felt this was easy, except for the issue I had on the night I was to test for my card.

The day before my CPR test I was stung by a bee on my right wrist. I didn't know it at the time but I was allergic to bees. Some gave me a local reaction, some affect my breathing. This was a yellow jacket, which gave me a local reaction and caused my arm to swell twice its normal size from my knuckles to my elbow. I looked like Popeye (the sailor man) but in only one arm. I went to class that next night, took my written exam, and passed. When it was time for me to take my practical exam, I showed the instructor my arm, and asked for an extension in time so I could do my demonstration when the swelling went down. He told me he'd observed my CPR skills from class and was satisfied I was competent. He asked me to show him where I'd place my hands, how many compressions would I do, and how many ventilations. Then he asked the same questions for a child and an infant. When he was satisfied that I was competent, he signed my paperwork. I had passed the CPR portion.

I'll be the first one to say that I don't normally do well on written exams. I read into questions, sometimes rush through and then making stupid mistakes. When the classroom portion was done, now came time for the final exam. One hundred questions on everything we'd learned over the last few months. I was a nervous wreck. I wanted this so bad. They say if you can answer the first question on a test with relative ease, the rest should be a breeze. We had three hours to complete the exam. When told to do so, I turned the page, looked at the first question and vapor locked! I don't remember the question, but I remember it stumped me for a moment. I closed my eyes, took a deep breath, and reread the question. I looked at the available answers and chose the best one. This went on for the first few questions, then things started coming back to me and the test got easier to handle. I walked away when I was done feeling unsure of my abilities and my efforts.

Two days later I did my practical exam. This was, again, a demonstration of everything we'd learned over the last few months. We had many different stations with skill tests. Each one came with a scenario and an evaluator, a stranger who was either a certified MRT or EMT. This person was now watching me to insure I did everything to state standards and followed protocols. Again, I was a nervous wreck. I nailed my practicals, passed every station.

Now I was waiting on my results from my written. My instructor said if we got a thin white envelope we'd failed. If a large manila envelope came, we passed. I remember coming home from school and finding a large manila envelope on the dining room table addressed to me from the State of Connecticut Department of Health. I screamed, tore it open to find my MRT card; a certificate; a blue patch that said State of Connecticut Certified with a blue star of life in the middle; and a separate purple patch to place above the CT patch that had MRT in big letters. I'd passed! I was officially a

Connecticut certified MRT. I was beyond excited. I wanted to sew a patch on everything I owned, I was that proud. The first time I was able to put my skills to the test would be the most memorable for me. It would also burn a memory in my brain that still lasts to this day.

Jamie

I remember it was a warm, humid summer night. I was on summer vacation from high school, getting ready to start my senior year. I was asleep in my bed when the fire radio in the kitchen alerted, "Motor vehicle accident with injuries, Route 85, south of your station." I jumped out of bed, dressed in record time, and was out the door. The captain of the fire department was my neighbor, so I ran to his house and rode with him to the station. I got into the rescue truck and we proceeded to the crash. The accident was less than half a mile south of our station. I got out of the rescue and walked into a horrific scene.

The first thing I saw was a blue pickup truck facing south in the southbound lane. It looked to be leaning to the left, parked there like someone had just stopped and gotten out. As I approached it I remember seeing a blue and white cooler lying open in the road. A package of hot dogs that had been run over by passing vehicles lay next to it. I remember it smelled really bad. Proceeding into the scene more, I saw a Volkswagen Beetle sitting on the front lawn of a house. It looked like someone had backed onto the lawn and parked facing the roadway. The damage to this vehicle was tremendous. The driver's side front end had been pushed all the way back to the driver's door. The roof was lifted up and also pushed back. The driver's door was now crushed and half its original size. As I surveyed the scene I noticed another vehicle off the road in the northbound lane. This vehicle looked very familiar. It was a silver Ford Granada. My brother owned a silver-colored Ford Granada. He worked in Groton and would have been coming home around this time. My heart sank. I remember feeling shaken and scared. As I stood there in shock, I could hear someone calling my name. As I came back to reality, I realized they were shouting my name and it was coming from the house. My brother stood in the doorway yelling my name. I felt instant relief. I wanted to run over and hug him. I ran to the house. He told me he had a female in the house with severe facial lacerations from the windshield and he needed a med kit and an EMT. I quickly ran to the rescue and got the med kit. As I went back, I informed the captain of what my brother said. I handed off the kit to him and went to assist at the scene in any way I could.

I found an EMT assisting a female patient who was lying on the ground next to the passenger side of the VW. I assisted him treating her and stabilizing her for transport to the hospital. Soon a stretcher arrived, we placed her on it and she was taken to a waiting ambulance. As I went back to the scene, I noticed the pickup truck was empty. I asked one of the police officers where the driver was. He informed me the driver fled the scene and they were actively looking for him. He then asked me if I could assist him in retrieving the driver's identification from the VW. As I reached into the car, I noticed the silhouette of a person in the drivers seat. I stopped and stared, wondering why nobody had cared for this person. I looked back over my shoulder at the police officer and he said she was deceased. My first dead body.

Sounds cold the way I just said that but that's what I felt that night. As I reached for the bag sitting next to her, I was able to get a good look at her. I knew her! I handed the bag to the officer, knelt down next to the passenger door and stared at the girl. I did know her. She was a classmate of mine. We were supposed to be starting our senior year together in a few months. As I looked at her, I couldn't help but notice that her hands still gripped the steering wheel. She looked like she was still driving except her head was laid back against the driver's seat. I was frozen. My first fatal accident and it was someone I knew.

The remainder of that night is mostly a blur. I remember it happened around 1:30 a.m. I spoke briefly with my brother. He told me who he was treating in the house, the sister of my classmate, and who the girl was that I helped. I think I walked around in a daze for most of the time. My department didn't have the Jaws of Life, so they contacted a neighboring department that did, and had them respond to assist us in removing her from the vehicle. Nothing could be done until the medical examiner arrived. The ME at the time was a crotchety old man (that's just my opinion) and hated being brought out in the early hours. I was standing near the VW when he approached to examine the driver. I was close enough to hear him say, "Yeah, she's dead."

I reacted with, "Really asshole, ya think!" Needless to say, I was quickly escorted away by fellow firefighters. I explained that I knew her and his attitude towards her offended me. I didn't say it as nicely then as I do here, but I hope you get the idea. Shortly after he pronounced her deceased, the Jaws of Life went to work removing her door. Once that was done, she was removed from the vehicle, placed on a stretcher, taken to the ambulance and transported to the morgue. We left the scene after both vehicles were towed away. The ride to the station was silent.

Once back in the station, a couple of senior firefighters pulled me aside and tried to talk to me. I remember them saying things like, "Shrug it off," and "Let it roll off your back." They told me if I didn't do this, it would affect me for the rest of my life and I'd probably quit if I let it get to me. I didn't know any better and these guys were my mentors. So that's what I did, I shrugged it off.

The first day of senior year, the principal made an announcement about the accident and the death of my classmate. People cried and hugged each other. I didn't tell anyone who knew her that I was there. I didn't want them to visualize what I saw. I knew they would ask.

That year, we dedicated our yearbook to her and her memory. This was the start of my pushing feelings down and keeping them in.

I used to laugh and joke about saving the world when I first started in the Fire Service. This, I'm pretty sure I can say with surety, is when the laughter died. This was the start of PTSD.

Two For The Show

One of the bad things about PTSD is not knowing you have it. If I would have known, then I could have taken steps to get treatment for it right away. Instead, my life went on and I stayed doing things with full enthusiasm. I stayed very active in the fire department, attending fire school, working bingo at the FD and generally waiting until the next call came. Little did I know that three weeks later my young mind would again be subjected to trauma and death.

The summer of 1979 was especially warm. Days were hot, nights were humid. This night was no different. Again, as I lay asleep, the radio in my dining room came alive. "Motor vehicle accident, car into the pond, Route 85 and Route 161." This location was even closer to the station, less than .2 miles away. In fact, you can see this intersection from the fire house. It's a "T" intersection with a sizable pond on the northbound side of the road.

I shot out of bed, dressed, and ran to my neighbor's house to catch my usual ride to the station, only this time we went right to the scene. Arriving, I remember seeing a couple of cars stopped in the northbound lane next to the pond where the post and wire guardrail used to be. Walking closer, I noticed one of the vehicles belonged to a state trooper. His lights were flashing but his car was empty. I glanced over to the pond and there was a car on its roof across the other side, approximately 80 feet away. I saw the trooper standing next to the car. I yelled to him and he frantically waved me over.

I quickly ran around the side of the pond to where he was. The driver's door was open and he was standing in waist deep water with his hands inside the car trying to find the driver. He located him and together we pulled this man from the vehicle and laid him on the bank of the water. His face was deep blue. As soon as we placed him on his back, a flood of water came out of his mouth and nose. The trooper informed me there was another occupant inside. By this time, more help had arrived, and the others were attending to our first victim. The trooper and I, with our hands inside the car, eagerly searched for the other victim. I felt something brush past my hand, retraced my movements and felt another person's arm. Together we grabbed onto this arm and tried to pull, he wasn't moving. We figured he was trapped inside by something. Reaching in deeper, the trooper located the victim's belt line and began tugging. After what seemed like an eternity, we freed him, and were able to remove him from the car. He also released a large quantity of water from his mouth and nose. Both were deceased. Looking at them, they couldn't have been more than 22 years old each.

I was exhausted. I sat down on the edge of the pond with my knees drawn up to my chest. The trooper came over to me, placed his hand on my shoulder and said, "We did our best." But did we? Could I have done more? I'll never know. As I sat there taking in my surroundings, I observed a vehicle partially submerged, upside down in the pond, with two dead bodies lying next to it.

It wasn't until I looked in opposite direction that I noticed the house and people standing at the edge of the pond. They were just staring at us, then one of them yelled, "Are they dead?" The trooper nodded his head yes. That's when they unleashed a volley of derogatory comments our way. Apparently, they came out of the house immediately after the accident happened and could hear splashing coming from inside the car followed by yells for help. So these people started yelling at us because we didn't get there sooner: they were alive, we're useless scum and so on. Well, this was apparently more than the trooper needed to hear. He walked up to them and in the most polite way he could at the moment, asked them to go back into their home and wait for an investigator to come and speak with them. They, of course, denied his request. He then told them to stop shouting at us and he didn't see them in the water trying to perform any rescues. Their response? "It's not our job, it's yours." That comment has stuck with me since.

Hours later, the medical examiner arrived. He refused to trek down to where the bodies were, so we had to place them into a stokes basket (a metal stretcher shaped like a toboggan with sides) and carry them one at a time to the edge of the roadway. He did his examination, pronounced them both deceased, covered them with sheets, shook some hands and left. This time, instead of loading them in an ambulance for transport to the morgue, we waited for two vehicles from the funeral home to accomplish this grim task. While we waited, I remember it being very humid. The bugs were horrible and I stunk of pond water and gasoline. I just wanted to go home, shower and get back into bed.

I had been in the fire department for a total of 12 months and I'd already seen a lifetime of horror. Two fatalities in less than one month. I remembered what I was told, shrug it off. I tried, I really tried. The sad thing is, I remember the nightmares. These two guys were sitting up on the bank of the pond, water streaming out of their eyes, nose and mouth while they tried to talk to me. It really freaked me out. Eventually those stopped just like all the others had stopped, locked away in my brain to be released at a later date when I was not so prepared for them. Memories to come out at the most inappropriate times. My cup, as my therapist would say, was filling rapidly.

EMT

It was time to step up my game. I had followed all my steps according to plan. (No specific plan, just one I had set for myself.) Now it was time to become an Emergency Medical Technician. I approached the chief and got approval for the company to pay for it. I was excited to get started with the next chapter in my life.

The class was held in the firehouse. I was very happy to see that my instructor was a well known EMT and a friend of the family. This man had a reputation of being one of the best instructors in the area as well as a highly respected EMT.

I quickly learned that this was going to be tough. Things I needed to know were much more in depth than anything I'd taken up to this point.

The very first class started like all the others: instructor introduction, class syllabus, dates, times and locations. Then we started into legal aspects, things EMTs needed to know as well as laws that we had to follow. We learned who we could treat and who we could not. The difference between implied consent (when a person was unconscious and would probably want us to help) and verbal consent, when a person asked us for help. Refusals—who could refuse and who could not. Duty to act, when we saw an emergency or were at the station when an emergency happened we have a duty to act and help. Abandonment, when we are treating a patient and we walk away from them without anyone of equal or higher qualifications there to continue treatment. There were so many other things on the legal aspect. These are just a few and the definitions are very general. There was so much to learn just on legalities, I didn't know what else to expect.

We started into other chapters of our books. I learned all about the heart, the different chambers, how they worked, which ones supplied blood to the body and which one received. I learned the different pulse points on the body, how to take a blood pressure and determine different lung sounds and what they might indicate.

In both my AFA and MRT classes, we learned about fractures and how to splint them. With EMT, I learned the different types of breaks and what could cause them. We went into detail with the skeleton, muscles and skin and the different types of injuries each one could incur. We studied the different types of shock and what causes them. Seizures and what could cause them. Psychiatric emergencies and how to handle them. Bleeding control, wound care and dressings. We did vehicle extrication, taking injured people out of vehicles using the Jaws of Life. Backboards, when and how to use them. When we got to backboards, my instructor also incorporated water rescue and drowning. We went to the submarine base and utilized their pool for this. It was indoor and the class started in mid fall. We were instructed on the proper use of backboards to remove patients from water situations. We also practiced mouth to mouth on a rescue mannequin while still in the water. This was, by far, the best classroom so far.

Then came the chapter I was not looking forward to, childbirth. I wasn't sure I was really ready for this. We had classroom instruction on the subject as well as watching a movie of an actual live birth. We were taught on what to do if complications arose like a breech birth, when an arm or leg came out first. Prolapsed cord, when the umbilical cord presented first and what to do for excessive bleeding. I was very happy when we completed this chapter.

Every certification comes with a written exam as well as a practical exam. My written was the typical 100 questions with three hours to do it. I don't remember exactly how long it took me, but I do remember sweating through it. My practical was much different than ones before. A lot more stations, 10 or 11 I believe, and more entailed. Some stations I did with a partner and some I did solo. I felt I did okay when I was done.

As with other state exams, if I got a manila envelope in the mail, I passed. If I got a letter, I failed. Well, I received a letter. It said I had passed my practical exam, however, I scored a 68 on my written. I needed a 70 to pass. I was devastated. I contacted my instructor and he said I could retake the written in a few weeks. I studied like I never studied before. After a few weeks I retook my exam. This time I passed. I was a Connecticut state certified Emergency Medical Technician.

By the time my card and patches arrived, I had a few weeks as an EMT before going into the Military. I had joined the United States Air Force and was leaving for basic training on August 4, 1980. My enlistment lasted six years and I returned to Connecticut. Unfortunately, my certification was only good for two years so I had to retake the whole class again when I got out. This time, I passed on the first shot. Practice makes perfect I guess.

Dispatch

When my military enlistment was up, I returned home. I had to acclimate myself to civilian life so I did what I felt I needed to, I got right back into the fire department. Then it was job searching. I went back to the job I had when I enlisted, working in a welding supply warehouse. While on a day off, I stopped by the fire dispatch center to see if they were hiring. I left my name and number with the senior dispatcher and left. A couple of days later he contacted me and said I could start training for part time. I wanted full time but this was a start.

The night I started training I was to be with a seasoned dispatcher who I'd known for years. The shift I was training on was the night shift, 6 p.m. to 6 a.m. I was only to be there until midnight. I did some dispatching in the military as a police officer, plus I had a working knowledge of the fire department, its procedures and protocols.

I walked into the dispatch center, which was in our local police department, and was greeted by my trainer. He asked a few basic questions, showed me the procedure manuals and how the radios and tone board operated. He handed me the general procedure book and said I should read this cover to cover. It explained how to dispatch the fire department and ambulances to calls and what to do for all other emergencies. He then walked to the doorway and said, "I'll be in the kitchen if you need me." Thankfully the kitchen was just down the hall, but it felt like I was in a "sink or swim" situation. Hopefully I didn't sink!

I read the general procedure book at least three times that night. There were also four individual procedure books for each of the four departments in town. Each fire chief had individual procedures for their departments for certain situations. It was a little confusing at first but over time I understood it.

Then it happened, the emergency line rang. My heart raced, my hands got sweaty and I got really nervous, all in a matter of seconds. I answered the phone in the most professional manner I could. The person on the other end needed an ambulance. I asked all the basic questions, name, address and what the problem was. After I had all the info I needed I ended the call and alerted the appropriate fire department ambulance to the call. I felt really good. I can do this, I said to myself. The ambulance signed on the radio. When they arrived at the scene, I documented the times on the radio log. The emergency line rang again. Another ambulance was needed in a different part of town. Again, after all the questions I dispatched the ambulance for that district. Now I was tracking two active calls. I was getting lots of experience right away, but I wasn't done yet. For the third time in less than 45 minutes, the emergency line was ringing and I would soon be dispatching another ambulance for a medical call. Now I'm tracking three calls, typing three reports, answering the routine telephone line and trying to catch up on my reading. My trainer walked back into the office, inquired how I was doing and asked if I needed any help. When I said that I was all set, he smiled, turned and left the room. The rest of my time there was pretty uneventful. I finished my reports, updated the radio log and finished my reading. When midnight came, I said goodbye to my trainer and left the building. The next day I was contacted by the senior dispatcher. He told me he was informed about my training the night before. I apparently impressed my trainer because the senior dispatcher asked if I was comfortable enough to go on my own. When I said I was, he offered me my first solo shift, a Saturday night shift, 6 p.m. to 6 a.m. I was elated and scared to death all at the same time. After doing three years as part time, a full time slot opened up and I was offered the position. Needless to say I took it. It was one of the best moves I ever made.

Firefighter-1

I threw myself back into the fire department and started qualifying on the apparatus. At the time, the department I belonged to had two pumpers, a brush truck, a rescue truck and an ambulance. It took just about 10 months but I got through them all and soon was qualified.

To advance in this department, you need to be qualified on all apparatus. My goal was to run for lieutenant. Meeting night came and went. I was passed over for the position and it was given to someone who wasn't qualified. The chief approached me and told me to take this gentleman out on the trucks and get him trained. Being as angry as I was, I refused. I spent many hours and many days off working my way through the vehicles, following protocols and guidelines, to get myself in a position to run for an officer spot. I turned and walked away. It sounds very childish now but then, it was all principal.

I lasted another year at this department. Then, due to mismanagement and personal reasons, I left there for another department in town. I was welcomed in, introduced to all the members and immediately taken through the vehicles to familiarize myself with all the equipment. I reviewed their by-laws and procedures and learned I needed to be certified as a firefighter-1. I asked the deputy chief about a class and he told me that since I joined the fire service prior to 1979 I was grandfathered into this certification. I asked if I could take the class anyway, just to have it. He enrolled me in the class which was held at my new station and he was the instructor.

Any certification I've achieved, I've earned and I'm very proud of that. It just didn't feel right to say I had it when it was only being given to me. This class was just a grouping of every course I'd taken to date dealing with firefighting, the National Fire Protection Association had created this for uniformed certification nationwide.

The first day of class was like all others, instructor intro and class syllabus. This was going to be more intense. Ladder placement and proper carrying, hose placement, streams and packing of hose on the engines, forcible entry into buildings using axes and halligan bars, ventilation by cutting holes in a roof, where to cut and why, when and where to break windows and the proper way to do it. I learned search and rescue of victims from buildings as well as salvage and overhaul. Salvage is when you save or try to protect property inside a building and overhaul is when you remove sheetrock or siding looking for hidden fires. Self Contained Breathing Apparatus (SCBA) care and maintenance as well as proper ways to use them and conserve air. We were all held to very strict standards and our instructors made sure we knew what we were doing before moving on to anything else.

Our class was required to attend a live burn. This is when we find a building, board up the windows, fill a room with hay and light it. Once the fire is going good, taking care not to burn the building down and contain it to one room, instructors take us in the building and observe us putting out the fire. Then we practice our forcible entry by prying open doors and windows. We did search and rescue and ventilation. This was tiring, dirty work and I loved every minute of it. I learned so much more in this class than I had in any other classes. I was very happy I decided to do this.

I passed this class with no issues. Now was time to start attacking the apparatus and get myself qualified. Doing that in this department proved to be easier for me than before. I had people calling me offering to take me out and get me trained. This department had more apparatus also. Three engines, a brush truck, a rescue truck, a 100' straight rear mount ladder truck, an ambulance and a boat. It took a little while longer but I eventually worked my way through them and was qualified.

That year I was elected 3rd lieutenant. My job was inventory on engine 3. I had to maintain a current list of equipment and maintain a maintenance log for the vehicle. We also had ambulance crew nights. From Sunday to Friday we were assigned a night to crew the ambulance. Mine was myself and another EMT. We saw many calls and experienced a lot together.

Each year that went by I was elected to a higher position. The last position I held was assistant deputy chief, which I held for one year. Being a chief officer was very challenging. I was so used to being a grunt on the fireground that it was difficult to change. I was rolling hose in the street one night after a structure fire when the chief approached and asked what I was doing. He pointed out at least three or four members standing around doing nothing. I told him I lead by example so when I do ask someone to do a task, I can tell them that I've done it before. I wouldn't ask anyone to do something that I wouldn't readily do myself. He smiled and walked away. Needless to say, the next company meeting was interesting. There were a few people who were reprimanded for allowing me to roll hose.

Career Goal Achieved

Being a 911 dispatcher was both challenging and rewarding. Hearing the anguish in callers voices would make my heart race. As time went by, I learned breathing techniques that helped me stay calm and gather appropriate information so I could send the help they required. This was effective in helping the caller calm down also.

Every once in a while I'd get a caller who would scream at me over the phone and no amount of encouragement would help them. I had a call one day for a possible cardiac arrest. A son had come home and found his mom face down on the living room floor not breathing and no pulse. I asked him to hold while I started the closest ambulance. When I got back on the line, he had hung up. I immediately called him back and attempted to give CPR instructions over the phone. He yelled obscenities at me, and said, "Get the damn ambulance here," and hung up on me. I won't lie, I started to get anxious, wishing the ambulance would sign on soon. When they did sign on I advised them that I attempted CPR instruction over the phone but the caller hung up on me. They acknowledged my information and proceeded to the scene. The caller called back again and was hysterical demanding the ambulance hurry. I informed him they were on the way and asked if he wanted to attempt CPR, that I could instruct him. He again hung up on me. I felt helpless! The ambulance arrived a short time later and the crew went to work. They called on the radio and requested the police, advising they would not be transporting, they had an untimely. An untimely death is someone who has been without a pulse and not breathing for a long period of time. The factors taken into consideration are skin color (either blue or grey), lividity (pooling of the blood in the body, it looks like bruising), and rigor (stiffening of the joints). Most or all of these must be present before a EMT can do a presumption. Only a doctor can do a pronouncement so the EMT calls the hospital, gives all pertinent information, and the doctor gives back a time of death. That is one of the hardest things, besides dealing with children, that an EMT has to face, telling a family there is nothing they can do for their loved one.

The dispatch center I worked in was in the police station. We had a small room and we usually worked alone. We would double up during natural disasters, blizzards and hurricanes. I preferred working nights, 6 p.m. to 6 a.m. Not many people were in the building and phones were mainly quiet unless there was an emergency. We monitored all fire alarms for town owned buildings and water treatment plant high and low level alarms for after hours. Soon after going full time, we started monitoring burglar alarms for town owned buildings, why, I don't know. The state police had monitored these before we took it over.

After eight years of dispatching, I was hoping a position would come available within the fire departments for a career firefighter. A couple of guys did leave so the job was posted. I applied and was given a interview. I figured since I was already a firefighter in town that I would have no problem. I met all the qualification and knew all the roads in town. Needless to say, I was wrong. These positions were given to others. I stayed on in dispatch for a couple more years. The Mohegan Tribe gained their recognition and construction started on their casino in town. The deputy fire marshal for my town was hired as the fire chief/fire marshal for the Mohegans. He advised me he would start hiring for the fire department on the reservation. I applied and waited. As I was waiting to hear from him, two positions opened up in the fire department in town. I applied there also. I had another interview with the town Public Safety Commission and was recommended for an interview with the mayor, a step I had not done in previous attempts. I was called for an interview with the Mohegan Tribe soon after this. I sat down with the fire chief, passed off all my certifications, answered a few questions and left. My interview with the mayor was different. He asked why I wanted to move to the fire department. I answered his question with enthusiasm and confidence. He then told me if he hired me for the fire department, he would need to find a replacement for me at dispatch. To me, this was obvious but I couldn't figure out why he was telling me this. After I left his office I sat in the parking lot for a few minutes and thought about our interaction. Then it hit me. If he hired me for the fire department, he needed to interview more people for my job. This was a task he didn't want to undertake, at least that was my impression. I immediately got angry. How dare he hold me up from advancement because I would cause him some inconvenience. I was determined I was going to fight for this job.

A week later I'm working a day shift at dispatch when I had a phone call from the fire chief of the Mohegans telling me I had the job if I wanted it. I didn't know what to say, I was excited and scared at the same time. Was my dream finally coming true, was I finally going to be a paid firefighter? I asked him to allow me to think about it. He agreed and asked that I let him know by the end of the day. I promised I would. After hanging up with him I called the person I always called when I needed advice, my dad. I explained to him how I really wanted the town fire department job but here was a paid firefighter position sitting in my lap. He told me to take the day, weigh the pros and cons of the job and make a decision. His last bit of advice was to think about where I'd be most happy. I thanked him and hung up. I had a lot to think about.

Just before noon the mayor stopped by dispatch, knocked on the door and came in. He closed the door behind him and sat down. He looked at me and asked if I was still interested in the full time position with the fire department. I told him I was and waited for the words I had wanted to hear. He sat back in his chair, folded his arms across his chest and said the job was mine if I wanted it. I had all I could do not to jump in his lap and hug the living crap out of him! I maintained my composure and told him to consider today my two week notice. He shook my hand, gave me a start date and congratulated me. I was over the moon excited, then it hit me. I had a job offer from the tribe on hold. I felt bad because the fire chief was a friend of mine and I felt like I was letting him down. I gathered my thoughts and called him back. I told him the mayor had offered me the job in town and that I was taking it. He accepted this with an understanding tone, congratulated me and wished me the best of luck. I thanked him and hung up. By the end of the day my face hurt so much because I couldn't stop smiling. I was going to be a career firefighter/EMT, a goal I had wanted since I was a kid. Now it was really happening. I couldn't wait to tell everyone.

My First Two Weeks

My first two weeks as a career firefighter I was placed with another career guy in the station I would be working at. During this time I was trained on the two engines, the rescue and the ambulance. We went over policies and procedures as well as response protocols. I spent many days driving around the response district learning streets and key locations for water sources. Being a rural fire department we didn't have hydrants; we had lakes, streams and ponds that were available to us for water supply. After my two weeks of on the job training, I was left on my own. My shift was Monday through Friday 7 a.m. to 5 p.m. I usually arrived for my shift at 6:30 a.m., ready to go. That excitement for my job still exists today.

In the town I work for, we have four fire departments. At the time I was hired, we covered all four stations with one career firefighter during those hours. Once I was comfortable at my station I traveled to the other stations to qualify on their equipment. Since I was already a volunteer at one station, working at another, I only needed to go to the other two stations for qualifications. That was done in a couple of months. Each station has their own specialty piece of equipment. One has a 100 foot ladder truck, one with a 2500 gallon tanker and one had a heavy rescue/lighting truck. Those took some time, but I conquered it.

My probationary period was one year. During this time I had requirements to fulfill. I completed them with months to spare, now I just had to keep myself out of trouble.

My one year anniversary came up quickly. On September 9, 1997, I was a full fledged career firefighter and an active member of the International Association of Firefighters. I wasn't a seasoned veteran but I wasn't a probie anymore either. A couple of years later, we added a second shift of firefighters, working from 9 p.m. to 7 a.m. and covering two stations from Sunday to Thursday. The town hired two more guys to cover these shifts. Now it was my turn to be the trainer. I worked with one of the new guys for two weeks during the day to get him qualified on the apparatus and to familiarize himself with the roads, then I spent one week with him on his shift, at night. He did very well and was soon left on his own.

A couple of months went by and the night shift firefighter asked if I would switch shifts with him. He said night shifts were straining his marriage. After discussing this with my wife, I swapped shifts with him. This would be one of the best moves I'd make.

I had two more day shifts to go before I switched to nights and so far, I had gotten away clean, no major calls. I had less than an hour to go in my shift when a call came in for a medical. The residence was located in the neighborhood across from the fire department so travel time was less than a minute. I pulled up with the ambulance, got out and retrieved the medical bag from the compartment. As I walked to the front door I passed by the large living room window and saw a woman lying on her back with a man standing over her doing CPR. I stopped for a second, staring at him and broke into a run for the door. I remember stopping just inside the door and looking at the woman.

Here was a middle aged woman, lying on her back. Her face was blue and her husband was pushing on her chest. The other thing about her was she weighed over 400 pounds. Why did that matter you ask? This means we're pushing harder on the chest to reach the heart. She also outweighs our stretcher at the time.

I immediately asked what happened. He told me he was in the bedroom getting dressed to go out when he heard a loud thud. He came out and found his wife lying on her back not breathing. I took over CPR from him and started compressions. As more EMTs arrived, I tasked them with manufacturing two backboards together as well as cutting down shrubs outside so we could back the ambulance up to the steps. Another EMT joined me, informed me that paramedics were started and asked what I needed. I asked him to take over compressions so I could tube her. At the time, we were using EOAs, Esophageal Obturator Airways, which would extend down the throat to just below the opening for the lungs. There was an inflatable balloon at the end of the tube to block the gastric juices that tend to flow upward during CPR. Midway down the tube were holes which, when lined up correctly, would deliver oxygen directly into the lungs. Inserting this tube was tricky. I had to tilt the head back almost as far as it would go, lubricate the end of the tube and blindly insert it into her throat. At one point the tube stopped moving, but I was only mid way down. I had a couple of guys lift her by the shoulders which let her head slide back even more and allowed me to insert the tube. I inflated the balloon and started breathing for her using a BVM which is a Bag Valve Mask. It has a large, squeezable bag that connects to the tube. When squeezed, it delivered oxygen to the patient, simulating them taking breaths. I switched with the EMT doing CPR and started compressions again, counting out loud so he knew when to squeeze the bag.

At one point I looked up. Standing in the entrance to the room was a little girl. She might have been 9 or 10, tears streaming down her face, watching me do CPR on her mother. My heart broke. I couldn't think about that. I had to concentrate on the task at hand. I told the guy doing ventilations to find the husband and have him come get his daughter. She didn't need to see us doing this. He quickly located him and the little girl was escorted outside to a friend's house.

It seemed like forever but the paramedics arrived before we could move her. One paramedic, who I knew very well, came over to me, squatted down and asked what I had. After filling him in on all my information, he left the room and went to my ambulance to contact the hospital. After a few minutes he returned, looked me in the eye and said, "The doctor called it, stop CPR." I felt defeated. I worked so hard trying to save this woman and some doctor on the other end of a radio calls it! I was pissed! I stood up, walked outside and just stood in the yard looking around. There were guys still tying two backboards together. My stretcher was in the back of a pickup truck, she would have been laid directly on the floor of the ambulance. I told them they could stop, CPR was terminated. I didn't know what to do with myself. I knew I had a report to write and no information to put on it. I didn't even know her name. I went back inside, found the husband, expressed my condolences and asked him to answer some questions about her name, date of birth, medications, allergies and medical history. I felt so cold asking all these but I needed this information.

As I left the residence, I saw the little girl again. She was coming across the lawn with another woman who I assumed was the neighbor. Our eyes met for a moment. I tried to look away but I couldn't. She looked so sad. Her eyes were red from crying. I was crushed. I got into the ambulance for the short ride back to the fire department. The police were now in charge of the scene. I completed my report and drove home. To this day I can still remember every detail of that day and I'll never forget the look on that little girl's face.

Rollover

My first few weeks on nights people started calling me white cloud. A white cloud is someone who has no calls or has dodged many bullets. A black cloud is someone you don't want to be around because he's running all the time and you'll never get any rest. My days as a white cloud would end in a big way very soon.

It was a couple of weeks after Christmas and there was still no snow on the ground, or whatever had fallen was melted away. The cold was definitely there though. I was hoping I wouldn't have to go out this night. I should've just kept my thoughts to myself!

Around 1 a.m., my dispatch line rang. The dispatcher was asking if a certain road was in my district or another company's. I informed him it was mine. He then told me he had one call only for a vehicle rollover with a report of a person pinned under the vehicle. My heart sank. I said I'd be on my way.

As I was putting on my turnout gear, he put the call out over the radio. My adrenalin was really pumping and I was running all kinds of scenarios through my head. Is this going to be as reported or was someone just overly excited, which happens more than one would think. Either way, I had no idea what I was going in to.

I arrived on scene and saw that a Ford Explorer had rolled onto its roof and was off the road with the front end balanced on the edge of a hill facing the road. As I exited the engine, I was approached by the volunteer captain who informed me that we did indeed have a female patient pinned under the overturned vehicle. I immediately got on the radio and started requesting additional rescues and resources. As I approached the side of the vehicle, I saw a pair of legs sticking out from under the vehicle. She was on her back with her torso, from the waist up, underneath the car. I went to the rear of the vehicle, got down on the ground and crawled under the overturned car. She was conscious and alert but was having trouble breathing due to the weight of the vehicle pressing on her chest. I was committed now. Being under an overturned vehicle is a little nerve racking but I wasn't leaving my patient. I could hear voices around me and I started calling for assistance. Someone knelt down next to me and put their hand on my leg. I asked them to get me as many oxygen bottles as they could and a non-rebreather mask, which is a oxygen mask with a reservoir bag under the face piece. He returned quickly with the mask and I placed it on her face. I did my best to calm her and evaluate her injuries while others worked to secure the vehicle from moving as well as setting up airbags to lift the vehicle off of her. A paramedic arrived and I filled him in on her condition. The only vital signs I could get were a pulse and respiration. Her arms were pinned under the car and I didn't have a whole lot of room myself to move around. He filled me in on the progress of the extrication. They were waiting for an additional rescue and tow truck to arrive to assist. I didn't know it at the time but the chief had assigned someone to assist in whatever I needed as well as watching the oxygen levels on the bottles we were using. The paramedic asked if I felt the medical helicopter was warranted. I told him I felt it was, so he requested it.

I had no sense of time being under that vehicle. The chief informed me that they were ready to start lifting the vehicle and to let him know if the patient's condition changed at any time. They started lifting the rear first, then the front, alternating between the two in a slow fashion. It must have been taking a while because before I knew it the flight nurse from the medical helicopter was there and asking me questions about the patient. It takes the helicopter at least 20 minutes to get to us. After what seemed like an eternity, my patient's arms were free and she said she could breathe better. Taking a flashlight, I started looking around her for any other obstructions. What I found just added to the already difficult extrication. The vehicle had a luggage rack and somehow, her right leg was trapped between the roof of the car and the luggage rack. Now I had another problem, how the hell was I going to get her out of that. I called out for another set of eyes to look at this and help me figure out a method of removal. The paramedic crawled under with me and together we figured the best thing to do was dig under her to lower her down more and try to pry the luggage rack from around her leg. While others started digging, I called for the Jaws of Life spreaders. I was going to place the tip of the spreaders between the roof and the rack and slowly pry it open and remove her leg. I asked her if she felt any pain there and she said no. After a quick examination, I determined her leg wasn't broken and could easily be removed once this operation was completed. The jaws arrived and with much difficulty, I got the tips right where I wanted them. I slowly opened the tips. The luggage rack reached its breaking point and popped off, her leg was free. Now the others were able to slowly remove her from under the vehicle and onto a backboard. I quickly came out from under the car and went to my patient. She was being attended to by the flight nurse and the paramedic. As I got to her side, she reached up and took my hand and smiled. She thanked me for not leaving her. I told her she was getting a ride in a helicopter to the hospital and she'd be okay now. She insisted I ride to the helicopter with her so I did. Once on her way to the trauma center, I returned back to the scene. Looking at the car, I saw why the process took so long. There were ropes tied from the rear axle to trees surrounding the vehicle. A tow truck was backed up to the front of the vehicle, its cable attached to the front axle to stabilize the front. Airbags and wooden blocks were on both sides for lifting. Total extrication time was 90 minutes. I was on my belly under this car for an hour and a half. My body was sore after I relaxed, why, I didn't know. Maybe was my adrenaline that kept me going and now was calming down. After making the rounds thanking everyone, the chief approached me. He said he was going to pull me out from under the vehicle about half way through the extrication. I informed him he'd have had a hard time getting me out of there. Once I make patient contact I don't leave my patient, period!

We had a lot of equipment to pick up. It took almost as long to pack everything away as it did to rescue her. Once back at the station I received a phone call from the paramedic. He said he'd heard from the helicopter crew that the only injury my patient had was a broken femur (thigh bone). I thought, "How lucky could one person be." I was very happy she wasn't hurt worse, thanked him for the information and hung up.

We train for situations like this on a regular basis, however, they never happen the way they do in training. Go figure!

How Nightmares Are Made

Summertime in Connecticut is usually pretty warm and comfortable. One summer we had was especially hot. If I remember correctly, we had a week or more of temperatures above 90 degrees with high humidity.

I was returning from the hospital in my ambulance when dispatch came over the radio and asked my location. I informed him I was near the high school. He then dispatched me to a house near the lake for an unresponsive person, possible cardiac arrest. I told him I was responding. He acknowledged me and said he'd be starting a paramedic. I proceeded to the location, lights and siren, working out a game plan with my partner. He was to grab the med bag while I went in to evaluate the situation. The ride took us approximately 5-6 minutes.

Arriving on scene I noticed an older man waving us down. Now, anyone in the fire service or EMS field knows when family members meet you in the road it's never a good sign. Their excitement is sometimes over the top, but in this job you can't let their actions and appearance interfere with how you approach a situation.

I walked up to him and asked what happened. He stated it was his wife and she was in the house. He then turned and opened the door. Without exaggeration, the wall of flies that flew out was shocking, to say the least! They took up almost half of the door length. I had to duck going inside. Once inside it hit me. The smell was awful. I looked around the best I could. All the windows were closed tight and the shades were pulled closed, the only light was from the open door. There were paper bags full of garbage lining the wall to my left and looked to continue around the room and down the hallway. The heat inside this house had to be well over 100 degrees, I could hardly breathe due to the smell and heat.

The man walked toward a hallway, looked over his shoulder and asked that I follow him to his wife. I did so with much apprehension. I asked him to turn on a light so I could see but I don't believe he heard me because one never came on. I didn't have a flashlight with me either—didn't think I'd need one. I was tripping on bags of garbage during my trek down this dark hallway until we reached another doorway. I assumed it was one of the bedrooms. The man had entered the room ahead of me. I asked him to please turn on the light so I could help his wife. When he did, my heart stopped dead (no pun intended).

There in front of me was a bed. On the bed was a full human skeleton. The skull was exposed, eyes no longer there. What skin was left had decomposed and melted into the mattress around her. Her shirt was open, exposing what was left of her rib cage and spinal column. Where her internal organs should have been, mainly her liver, was a mound of thousands of maggots feasting on the remains. Her pants were still on, one leg on the bed and one leg in a pile of bones on the floor. I was in shock. I screamed like a schoolgirl (I apologize for the analogy), looked at the man, and in a loud, high pitched professional tone said, "What the fuck is this!" He told me that it was his wife. I asked when he spoke to her last and he replied, "last night." Obviously he didn't have a conversation with her last night so I told him to get out of the room. At this time, the rest of my crew was coming into the room. I ordered everyone out of the house and declared the house a crime scene. Once everyone had exited the residence I closed the door behind me.

Outside, I didn't know how to handle what I had just found. I was in shock. Just then, I saw the fire chief come around the corner. I got on the radio with dispatch, canceled the paramedic and requested the police respond. I then approached the chief and asked him if he wanted to come see what I just found in this house. After looking at my expression and the obvious smell coming off of me, he politely said, "No!" I turned and walked away.

I had one of my guys back the ambulance into the driveway. I knew the police would be needing masks and gloves to go inside so I had them ready to go on the rear step. The first state trooper to arrive came up to me and asked what I found. I explained the scene to him and offered him a surgical mask, explaining the smell was overpowering. He smiled and refused the mask. I remember saying to myself, "Okay, John Wayne, you go right ahead!" He wasn't in the house more than 30 seconds and he was back asking for a mask. I just smiled and handed him one.

Pretty soon detectives arrived it was determined that the husband needed to be transported for a psychological evaluation. This man had spent many days with this corpse and the smell was outrageous. I put on a full body biohazard suit before getting in the ambulance. We transported him to the local emergency room. Once we arrived, we took him inside. The nurses started to laugh when they saw my attire. Their laughter abruptly stopped when the odor hit them. I filled them in on the situation and he was placed into a treatment room. A doctor entered the room, took one look at the man and ordered that his clothing be removed and sent to the incinerator and he be cleaned up and fed. A nurse removed the man's shoe and a pile of live maggots fell out. I looked at the maggots, then at the nurses, shook my head and left the room. I think I washed my hands and face 10 times before I left the hospital. I felt gross.

I returned to the fire house and fully decontaminated the ambulance from top to bottom, inside and out. I swear I could smell that for weeks after. Once you smell death, it's an odor you never forget or get used to.

Later that day, I received a phone call at the station from dispatch. He said the M.E. was at the residence and refused to go inside without an SCBA. I didn't blame him. I had about 5 guys at the station who readily volunteered to go and assist. I'd seen enough so I sent them along. I wasn't eager to step foot near that house anytime soon.

When they returned, they cleaned and refilled the SCBA's that were used. One of them told me he assisted the M.E. with the removal. They decided the best way to remove the body was to take the bed linen also. So, they wrapped her in the bed linen and removed it from the bed. He told me when the linen came off, it sounded like peeling Velcro. I was very happy I didn't go now.

After this call, the nightmares started big time. I had dreams of her sitting up in bed and talking to me, chasing me and just plain old scaring me. I was afraid of the dark as a child but overcame that in my early teens. All my hard work was now shot to hell. I couldn't walk into a dark room for years after this call. My brothers used to tell me about the boogie man. I'd heard stories about the boogie man as a child. Once I was an adult I realized the boogie man wasn't real, WRONG! The boogie man became very real for me and became alive in my brain on this day. It took many, many sessions with my therapist to kill this thing again. I still, to this day, have problems walking into a dark room but it's getting better.

When The Laughter Dies

After my run in with my boogie man, that's when my issues started. The nightmares I had after that incident were almost childlike. I'd be on a call and I'd enter a dark room with a skeleton. She would sit up, talk to me, chase me and just generally scare the living hell out of me. Little did I know, this was the start of PTSD rearing its ugly head.

PTSD (Post Traumatic Stress Disorder) is a very nasty thing that affects not just military combat veterans, but firefighters, EMTs, paramedics, police and all first responders who deal with death, destruction and high stress situations. Actually, anyone who's had a traumatic experience in their life is subjected to the possibility of this condition. For me, it affected my sleep (couldn't close my eyes without seeing my boogie man) and my eating habits (I either ate too much or no food at all). My personality? I kinda became an asshole to everyone, except our children and our pets. My wife and co-workers were my biggest targets. I had no patience for anyone or anything. There would be days I could find something wrong with just about anything. One day we were headed to the beach. It was a beautiful, sunny and warm summer day. My wife drove as I watched out the window. As we got closer to our destination I saw a stray cloud in the sky and that was it, the day was ruined, it was sure to start pouring down rain and destroy any hopes of me having fun! It was one cloud! That's how deep I was into this and didn't realize it.

What brought everything to a ugly head was a call I had which changed my life forever. This one call sent me into a downward spiral which lasted almost two years prior to seeking treatment. This is the one call that almost ended my career and almost ended me.

EC-33, Officer Down

The way our shifts worked we had three man coverage at night from 9 p.m. to 7 a.m., one guy in three out of four stations. I was working Co-1 or Company One. It was Monday September 6, 1999. There were a few volunteers hanging around the station with me. It was getting late in the evening, I think around 11 p.m. when dispatch called on the direct line. (Dispatch would call to pre-notify us of EMS calls.) I answered the phone and the concern in the dispatcher's voice made me nervous.

"I received a call from [insert address here] reporting two gunshot victims. How do you want to handle this?"

I told him to alert Co-1 and Co-2 EMS people and start two medics. I ran upstairs to the apparatus floor yelling for a driver to come with me. We departed the station, lights and sirens, to our destination. Enroute, dispatch notified me that the police were responding but not on scene. I advised him to have all incoming EMS units stage approximately 2-3 blocks from the scene until we were cleared to come in. We arrived in the staging area and parked on the side of the road. This road was rural with woodline on both sides.

As we waited, police car after police car sped past with lights and sirens blasting. It seemed like an eternity, but we were called into the house finally. Driving up to the scene it looked like something out of a movie. Police cars lined both sides of this neighborhood street. The house was easy to find. Myself and Co-2's ambulance arrived at the same time. I backed into the driveway and they backed in next after us. I told my partner I was headed in to evaluate the situation. On my way in, I passed a police officer I'd known for years.

As I passed, I asked, "What do we got?"

He never looked at me. He kept his head down and said, "Just get in there!"

His words didn't hit me at the moment, but they would later.

As I walked in the front door of the residence, the stairs leading to a lone bedroom were on the left. I saw a police officer at the top of the stairs. As I went up I noticed his expression. I couldn't tell at the time if it was shock or sadness.

As I entered the bedroom, I entered into a life-changing hell. I had two victims of GSW (gunshot wounds). The first person I saw was a male, lying on his back with his arms at his side and his eyes closed. I felt his neck for a pulse, one was there. I noticed a hole with a burn mark under his chin, GSW. I started feeling around behind his head looking for an exit wound–there was none. He wasn't breathing. I walked around the other side of the bed to a female lying next to him. She had a open GSW to the left temple area of her head. She had agonal respirations (deep breathing about 4 times a minute). I checked the opposite side of her head for an exit wound, none! At this point, the room flooded with EMTs and two paramedics. Everyone started working at once, now I was in the way. I told one of the medics I was going downstairs to the ambulance to call the hospital and request a double trauma alert and give them a brief description of what to expect.

Once outside I noticed that both stretchers were set up at the doorway and two backboards were making their way into the house. I climbed into the patient area of my ambulance, grabbed the med radio and notified the hospital of our situation. At this point, I was greeted by one of the neighbors asking what was happening. I told him to return to his property without giving him what he asked for. Being the nosy neighbor he was, he asked again in a more firm tone. I had had it with him at this point, I snapped! I started yelling at this man to remove himself from my general area or I would bodily assist him in doing so!

I turned and walked back to the house just as the male was being carried down the stairs. He was intubated and someone was breathing for him while another person was doing CPR. We placed him onto the stretcher and moved him to the first ambulance. I walked back to the house. The female was already on my stretcher and being moved to my ambulance. She, also, was intubated and CPR was being performed. I took over ventilations. While enroute to the hospital my partner, who was doing CPR, asked if I knew who the male GSW victim was. I said I didn't (I really didn't stop to look or notice).

He said, "It's Chip."

My heart exploded in my chest. Chip was a police officer in town and one of my really good friends. I couldn't think about it at that moment. I had a job to do, his girlfriend was relying on me to breathe for her. We arrived at the ER and were met by a trauma team who whisked her away from us and continued life saving measures.

I went in search of my friend. He wasn't hard to find. Stationed outside the room he was in were two state troopers. Thankfully, I knew them both, so they didn't stop me from walking into his room. I walked in and stopped cold! Here was my friend, lying on this hospital bed, no life saving measures being done. He had paper bags attached to his hands to preserve any evidence or DNA belonging to the bastard who did this. I stood there, I'm guessing in shock, and just stared at him. I remember saying to him how sorry I was that I didn't recognize him. My heart was broken. My friend was dead and I couldn't do a damn thing to help him. I was also angry because an unknown person had killed someone I was close to. I turned and walked out of the room stopping at the troopers to inquire what had happened.

What they told me sent chills down my spine and rage through my body. Chip's girlfriend had an ex who was a loose cannon. This ex apparently entered the house through the rear door, walked past his children, who were awake watching TV, and walked upstairs. He placed a 9mm automatic under Chip's chin and pulled the trigger. When Chip's girlfriend, the perpetrator's ex, raised her head in shock, he shot her in the temple. He then walked calmly down the stairs and out the front door.

Rage had set in solidly now. I wanted this person to feel the pain I was feeling. I walked outside the hospital and started pacing the parking lot trying to make sense of all that had just happened. I did this for awhile before walking back in and checking on my patient. That's when I overheard the troopers talking to each other. They said the shooter was located. He had driven to an area north of us and attempted to commit suicide by shooting himself in the stomach. An ambulance was transporting him to the hospital we were at.

Here was my chance to confront this asshole. My partner asked if I was ready to leave and I informed him we weren't going anywhere until this ambulance arrived. We exchanged a few words, him trying to convince me that it was in my best interest to leave and me telling him to perform an impossible sexual act upon himself! At this point, one of the troopers I knew heard our conversation and approached me. He said I should go before the ambulance arrived due to my connection with Chip. I requested he try the same procedure I had explained to my partner. Both of them now were trying to calm me. I was beyond angry, I wanted revenge for my friend. With much physical encouragement, I was placed into the passenger seat of my ambulance and removed from the hospital. I arrived back at my station and completed my report. I was told by my supervisor that it was okay if I wanted to take the rest of the shift off. I refused. I felt if I left now, I'd never return. I paced around the apparatus bays and outside for hours.

Around 6:30 a.m., I was told that detectives from the Connecticut State Police Major Crimes Division would be here to interview me, also, the Critical Incident Stress Debriefing Team would be arriving and I was to stay and attend. I called my wife to tell her I would be home late and the reason. At this point nothing had hit me emotionally. It wasn't until the first detective arrived, a female trooper I knew very well from my time as a state police dispatcher, that I fell apart for the first time. She reached out and held me as I cried uncontrollably, shaking and sobbing into her shoulder. Once I calmed, we went upstairs to the meeting hall and she proceeded with her interview. I had to relive all this horror for her in graphic detail. When she was done asking questions, I asked about the condition of the shooter. She advised me he was alive and being treated by the ER doctors.

A short time later, all who participated in this incident arrived as well as the CISD Team. We all proceeded to the meeting hall to begin our debriefing. The CISD Team is comprised of any or all of the following: doctors, nurses, psychologists, therapists and/or current or past EMS, fire or police personnel. These sessions are private and no one is allowed to observe unless you were involved in the incident.

We all arranged chairs in a circle and sat quietly. The lead person for the CISD Team spoke first and explained the rules: no judgments, no talking about this debriefing outside this room and honesty at all times. Each person took turns talking about the incident and how they felt at the moment. I was seated next to a female paramedic who I had been friends with for years. When it was my turn to speak, I broke. I started to cry uncontrollably again. She put her arm around me and held me. I felt so sad, so lost. My friend was dead, murdered by an animal, and I couldn't help him. I would never see him again, never hear his infectious laugh or see his smile. I was angry, no—I was pissed off! They came back to me two more times, each time was the same, I was crying too hard to talk. I just wanted them to leave me alone. When the session ended, the lead person pulled me aside and handed me a sheet with the list of symptoms to watch for called

The Seven Stages of Grief. I was instructed to take it home and share it with my wife. I did as I was told.

Chip's wake is a blur to me even today. I remember riding with the guys to the funeral home, seeing his cruiser parked out front with its overhead lights on but I'm blank about everything else. I don't remember going inside, seeing him, or anyone for that matter. It bothers me that my brain needs to protect me from this. I want to remember. Just now is not the time, I guess.

I had to work the day of his funeral but was able to attend anyway with the fire department. Police from all over showed up. It was standing room only inside as well as outside where I was. I remember it was a beautiful, sunny day. After it was over, I returned to the station, parked my rig, found a quiet, private place and cried as I remembered my friend.

I don't remember the time frame, but a short time later I found out that the shooter succumbed to his injuries. I remember feeling good about that and cheated at the same time. Bastard got off easy!

Now for the kicker. A few weeks went by and someone informed me that the shooter had sent a letter to the mayor informing him of his plan and an explanation as to why he killed the responders. *What?!* Apparently, he had planned to be hiding in the woods, just beyond where we had staged that night, fully armed. His intention was to shoot at and "take out" the ambulances and the personnel in them to prevent any aid from reaching the house. My only guess is he got cold feet and just ran.

Because the incident took place over the Labor Day weekend, the mayor didn't receive the letter until after everything had happened. When I first heard about the letter and his plan, it really didn't phase me, then after thinking about it, it scared the living hell out of me. Thinking about how close I came to dying that night just added to my already fragile emotions. Welcome to PTSD!

Intro-ducing... PTSD!

The next few weeks are mainly a blur to me. There were nightmares, anger, bouts of crying for no reason and anxiety. Suddenly, large crowds made me nervous. My family noticed a change in my behavior almost right away. I told my wife about the night Chip was murdered, what I saw and did, all without mentioning his name. I couldn't say his name and referred to it as "the incident." She was picking up on all the signs and symptoms that were listed on the paper I brought back from the CISD Team. I had them all! She tried to talk to me about seeing a professional. I fought her all the way. I was fine, or so I thought. After a few weeks she finally convinced me to call the woman from CISD. We made an appointment to come to her home where her office was located. I felt this was a waste of my time, I was fine.

The ride to her home was long and boring. I thought about what we would say to each other. As I located the address, I pulled my car into the driveway of a modest home in a residential neighborhood. I was apprehensive about all this, I was fine. I knocked on the door. The woman who opened the door was familiar to me—I remembered her from that day. She invited me in and offered me a cold drink. I refused, I was fine!

She led me through her home to a room that was bright and inviting. This room looked like an office. Book shelves lined two walls with a large desk, plants and comforting decorations. That's the best way I can describe it. She offered me a seat and closed the French doors that separated us from the rest of the house. We made small talk for the first few minutes. (I'm guessing to get me comfortable.)

She then pulled up a chair close to me, facing me. She put out her hands to me and I took them. In a soft voice she asked me to take her back to the night Chip died. I immediately choked up and began to cry, I wasn't fine! With gentle encouragement, she asked again. My crying became sobbing. She squeezed my hands, told me I was safe there, and asked again. I began to recall all events to her from beginning to end. When I was done, she reached out and hugged me and told me how proud she was of me. After a few minutes she asked me to tell her again, this time I was to use Chip's name. The second time was a little easier. As I was talking, she would gently squeeze my hands when she heard a change in my voice. We did this two more times until I could freely say Chip's name without my voice cracking. I felt relieved, freed of the demon that was riding me for the last couple of months. She told me to stay until I felt that I had composed myself enough to safely drive home. I thanked her for all her efforts. I smiled, genuinely, for the first time in a long time.

As soon as I got home, I told my wife all about it and retold the story using Chip's name. I felt great, better than I had in weeks. This relief would be short lived. I had only broken the surface and PTSD was about to come into full view.

PTSD Brain

Following the birth of our daughter in 2000, things had been up and down. I was arguing more. Everything pissed me off both at home and at work. I found myself clinging to our daughter and our cat: innocence that couldn't hurt me. Our son was my best buddy. Everyone else was the enemy.

This timeline is still all a blur to me. I don't remember a whole lot during this time. My therapist calls this PTSD brain (that's when my brain tries to protect me from myself and my past). The only thing I do remember, I was an asshole a lot of the time. Not on purpose, I just couldn't help it.

Weeks turned into months, months turned into years until my wife, again, convinced me to see a professional. I found a male therapist close to our home. I only saw him for a little while. Quite honestly, he creeped me out. The first thing he told me to do was label all my food, really! Our sessions consisted of me talking for 45 minutes while he sat there and stared at me, very rarely saying anything. Eventually I stopped seeing him. I felt I was getting nowhere fast.

I don't remember the amount of time that passed (again a blur) but I was in a really bad way. I was crying more often, arguing a lot and my anxiety was through the roof. I had to do something but I was afraid. I called my primary care doctor. He recommended a therapist group just down the street from his office, giving me the number and name.

I dialed the number. The auto answer with voice mail menu came on. I entered the number for the voice mail I wanted. As soon as the therapist's voice came on I lost it. I began to cry so hard I couldn't speak. My wife took the phone and left a message.

I was worse than I thought. I needed help. I felt like my world was crashing around me faster than I could stop it. I couldn't wait to get in this office and start relieving this hell I was in.

Timmy

Before I start into my therapy, let me take a moment and backtrack a little. The events leading up to therapy and my willingness to go were filled with turmoil, hurt and anger. I was reliving all my past calls. The problem was, I didn't know it. It was like a silent movie in my subconscious, replaying over and over again. My wife, kids, friends and family paid the price. I was a different man. The only ones who didn't suffer were my patients.

After Chip died, something inside of me snapped. My therapist would later inform me of the "glass half full theory." My glass was not only full, at this point, it was overflowing at a rate equal to Niagara Falls! Everything I had ever seen or been involved in, traumatic in nature, throughout my life and career, was rearing its ugly head all at once and my brain was trying to process it. That's a battle I was losing.

My wife is a very strong person who didn't sign on for this when we got together. We were married for two months when Chip died. For the next couple of weeks I walked around in a daze with my guard up, trying to protect myself from hurt. That would prove to be futile.

One of my best friends growing up was a friend my family had known for years. He was 20 years older than me but the biggest kid I knew. I spent many days at his house playing Yahtzee, Monopoly and other games. He was a mechanic by trade and taught me many things about fixing cars. We did a lot of things together, him, his wife and I. It would be them, later in years, who introduced me to my wife.

While I was away in the military, my dad informed me that my buddy had had a heart attack. My dad said he would be ok, just wanted me to know. I was scared for him. See, he was a smoker and when his doctor told him to quit, he didn't. Once I was out of the military, I resumed contact with him. I eventually moved into his home when my first marriage failed. Soon after that, I was introduced to my wife. She worked with my buddy's wife at the local grocery store. My wife and I moved into an apartment together soon after this and we lost contact with him.

Sometime along the way, I heard he had been diagnosed with lung cancer and had half of one lung removed. I tried to stop by his house on my way to work, but it didn't always work out. The few times I did stop, he was in pain. He looked like a different person. The guy I remember was active and always joking. Now he was inactive and serious, this proved more than I could deal with.

September 29, 1999, I returned home the morning after a shift to find my wife sitting on the back steps. She didn't usually wait outside for me, at least not this early in the morning. As I approached her, I could see the pain on her face. I don't remember if she told me or I guessed but my best buddy in the world had passed away. I was numb at first but then it hit me, another person I was close to had died. Next to set in was guilt. I should have visited him more, I should have been there for him more, I should have been by his side when he died! Damnit! Why are all my friends dying? This was three weeks after Chip. My brain was mush, my personality was damaged.

I don't remember his wake but his funeral was so hard. I cried through most of it. It was an overcast day outside, that I remember, because when we all left the church, the clouds opened up directly over us and the sunshine came through. He was smiling down on us. The graveside service was short and sweet. He was laid to rest next to his young son who was killed in a car accident in 1976. They were now together again. After this moment, I think my brain went on vacation. It had had enough.

The days, weeks, months and years that followed are jumbled in my brain. I remember some events but not all. I remember events but not a timeline of when they occurred. I just remember being sad a lot, arguing a lot, being angry a lot and withdrawing a lot.

The anger was the worst for me and my family. I told my wife early on in our dating that she would never want to see me really angry. Unfortunately she saw it more than I'm comfortable admitting to. See, when I got angry during early PTSD, things got thrown. Objects that were close to me were picked up and heaved as hard as I could. I broke two pair of glasses, a phone and countless other items.

Things got so bad that there were times my wife would tell our son that we were going somewhere and he would ask, "Does Daddy have to come?" I didn't find that little tidbit out until my wife came to me, very strong and firm, and told me if I didn't get help now that she and our kids were leaving! That was my wake up call. Again, I don't remember a whole lot about the events leading up to this point, but that one is very clear to me. That was what I needed. That started a chain of events that would bring me down a road to recovery.

Family Life

One of my biggest fears at this point is that this book probably reads as well as instructions on how to program an old VCR. I jump around a lot with events, unfortunately, that's how my brain works right now. I feel it's best to leave it this way to show exactly how a PTSD brain sees the world.

I function as well as anyone who doesn't have PTSD. Well, almost. I can dress myself, eat when I need to and do everyday things to survive. Crowds bother me. Most things that upset the stability of my life make me anxious. I'm learning to deal with those things daily. I'm better than I was but I have a long road ahead.

One of the hardest things I've had to do so far is write this book. I relive every incident with every chapter. I've cried through some and gotten angry through others.

The worst thing anyone can do is ask a firefighter, EMS provider, police officer or military member, "What's the worst thing you've ever seen or been involved in?" In essence, you're asking them to relive the worst horror they've ever been involved in. I usually tell people I've seen just about every imaginable way the human body can be damaged. If you're not prepared for the nightmares that follow, don't ask!

I've been told, "If it's so bad then don't do it anymore." I wish it were that easy. Everyone seems to think I chose to be a firefighter/EMT, I didn't. It chose me! I'm good at what I do. I'm excited to go to work everyday. After 37 years combined volunteer and career service, how many people can say that about their job. After all the crap I've seen, I still look forward to walking in that station with my head held high, waiting for whatever life throws at me during my shift.

The Fire Service is a family, a brotherhood/sisterhood. People who are not involved don't get it. That's ok, I do and so do my extended family members. The movie *Backdraft* first brought forward a saying that has been in the fire service forever, "You go, we go!" That is a code we live by. I have your back, you have mine. The best part is, we don't need to say it, it's there every time the alarm sounds for a call or when one of us is in personal turmoil, and this always happens without questions or scorecards for payback. That is a true family!

Therapy 101

The days leading up to my first appointment with my new therapist were filled with fear, anxiety and just not knowing what to expect. My wife was very supportive throughout this ordeal. Always by my side, offering to go with me and be there when I was done, but this was something I needed to do on my own. I'm one of those people who has gotten everything I have and gotten as far as I have without a lot of assistance. All my jobs I've achieved based on my merits, not by a "good word" being placed by someone, something I pride myself on. This I had to do without any help, or I wouldn't do it at all.

The day came when I was to meet my new therapist. I hoped and prayed this one was better than the other one, the "mark your food" one! He was my first impression of therapists and it was holding firm with me.

I arrived outside this modest house across the street from the hospital. I got out of my car, took a deep breath and entered the unknown. I climbed the stairs onto the wooden front porch. On the outside wall, to the left of the main door, was a list of the therapists and psychiatrists who worked inside. I found the name of the person I was to meet and thought to myself, "Please don't be a whack job!"

Again, after another deep breath, I reached for the door and walked inside. Closing the door behind me, I looked around and located the receptionist. I told her my name and who I was there to see, fighting back tears the whole time. She met me with a smile, and asked me to have a seat with a kind tone. My hands were sweating so bad I didn't dare pick up a magazine in fear I'd ruin it, and Lord knows I wouldn't have been able to concentrate. This woman came out of one of the rooms, approached the receptionist and leaned over her shoulder. She then looked up and asked if I was Paul. I only nodded my head, unable to speak because now the tears were really trying to beat their way out. She led me to one of the rooms, closed the door behind me and offered me to sit anywhere I wanted. The room looked like anyone's living room in their house. Comfy chairs, a desk with a telephone, bright open windows and decorations all over the room. It was a very comfortable environment. I had to chuckle to myself, she had a couch! What would a typical therapist's office be without a couch.

As we sat, she started with basic business questions, what insurance did I use, who did I work for, etc. Then she looked at me, which seemed honest and caring, and questioned me about my phone message and the fact that I melted down. I just remember bursting into tears, sobbing and trying to speak the best I could. I don't remember every detail of our first meeting, however, I do remember her being incredibly kind, soft spoken and encouraging. The hour, I remember, passed way too quickly.

At the conclusion, she advised me she wasn't "in network" with my insurance company. She recommended that I see another therapist who was in the group and was accepting of my insurance. She told me her name and said she was very good and could help me tremendously. I thanked her, opened the door and followed her to the receptionist. They were kind enough to set up my next appointment with the new person. I paid, thanked them both and walked to my car. Again, not all events I remember. But I do remember sitting in my car feeling some relief, mainly from knowing that I now have a resource to feel better. Some anxiety was still there because I was going to go through this all over again, meeting someone new. Little did I know I was about to meet the woman who would save my life!

The Road To Recovery

I remember trying to be positive, trying to stay optimistic and having it be very, very hard. After many sleepless nights, the day came when I was to meet my new therapist, again! I was scared now. I didn't know what to expect. I'd met so many new people in the last couple of weeks, it was a little overwhelming.

Anytime I left the house for a therapy session, my wife always had words of encouragement, "Good luck, you'll do fine." I carried those words all the way to my destination. Those words I repeated to myself over and over again as I drove, good luck, you'll do fine. Now if I could just convince myself that I'd do fine.

I arrived, stepped out of my car, and approached the office. I opened the door and walked into somewhat familiar territory. I approached the receptionist, smiled and let her know I was there and who I was seeing. She informed me I could wait upstairs. Upstairs? Uh oh! This is new. I was not sure I wanted to have anything else new. I was scared enough. My world had been turned upside down with all this new stuff.

I cautiously walked upstairs. At the top of the stairs, I was looking at the typical second floor of a normal house with, of course, a few exceptions. There were doors leading to rooms/offices. There was a small waiting area with four chairs and a table with magazines. I assumed this is where I was to wait. As I sat there looking around, taking in my surroundings, I started to notice things. Signs on the wall to please keep conversations to a low tone, therapy sessions in progress. There was a notice stating that this office required 48 hours notice for cancellations. I remember thinking, 48 hours? Really! What if something happened that morning and I couldn't make it? Was I still required to pay? I don't think so!

One of the doors opened and a woman entered the hallway. She smiled at me, asked if I was Paul, and invited me into her room. As I entered I noticed a bookshelf filled with an assortment of books, games and puzzles. She offered me a seat in one of the two chairs in the room. I remember thinking that this room seemed more business-like than the one downstairs. As I sat down, she sat across from me, smiled, and started off by asking the same questions the first therapist asked. After the business side was done, she asked me about myself. I told her about my personal life (a brief rendition) and about my job. She then asked me what brought me there. BOOM! I broke down. I didn't understand why I broke down so quickly. My guess is that she seemed comforting, honest and caring. I went on and on about Chip and the days and weeks that followed. She looked at me with sad eyes, leaning forward in her chair so she could hear every word I said. When I was able to take a breath, she interjected. She told me she was going to work with me slowly, going backwards and starting at my childhood and working our way forward but first, she was going to help me deal with the death of my friend. The rest of the session, I talked, cried and talked some more. When the hour was up, she suggested I consider coming two days a week. I wanted to come once a day but twice a week sounded good to me. I left that session feeling drained. I was exhausted and my head hurt. I was on the right track and I had the right person to get me there.

I arrived home and filled my wife in on my session. I was still a little apprehensive, but trying to be positive. I was ready to move forward. I couldn't wait until my next session. We were in the beginning of 2001. I had been a career firefighter/EMT for five years at this point.

Like anyone who suffers from PTSD, I had good days and bad days. The bad days seemed to come more often. My brain tried to protect me from so much that I don't remember, to this day, all the bad days I had. Some were filled with anger and some with sadness. I cried a lot, I raged a lot also. I argued about the stupidest stuff. I had to be right! The biggest target of my rage was my wife. During the height of my PTSD, she was the enemy. I questioned everything she did.

I remember there were days I didn't want to be touched and days I couldn't get close enough to her. The problem was, I never vocalized this to her. She was guessing every day on how my mood would be. My family was walking on eggshells around me and I could feel it. This made me feel anxious and guilty which added to my rage, mainly at myself, but also at her. Thankfully, never at my children. It shouldn't have been directed at her either but I couldn't control it, which also added to the rage and guilt. It's an awful feeling to hear hurtful words come out of your mouth and not have the ability to control them. I was out of control a lot of the time.

My wife would say things like, "Talk to your therapist, she'll tell you." That would make me mad. I knew she was right but, at that time in my life, I needed to be right. I felt like I was going down a road of no return. I had enhanced "fight or flight" symptoms. I would yell and scream, throw objects and yell more. When I felt I was losing the battle, I would grab my keys and leave the house, threatening to divorce my wife as I left. After a few hours of cool down time, I would return, calm, and ask for forgiveness. We would sit and talk calmly for hours after those incidents.

One of my biggest issues during this period was my lack of patience. The only difference, I wasn't this way at work. My bedside manner with my patients that I dealt with at work was still professional. I was a different person at work then I was at home. I was keeping a big secret from my coworkers. I felt if I told them the issues I was having dealing with Chip's death, they would see me as weak. I already saw myself as weak. What was wrong with me! I was stronger than this. I was a big tough firefighter, thinks like this don't affect us. I couldn't have been more wrong and I was about to find out just how wrong I was.

September 11, 2001

The morning of September 11, 2001 started like any other day for us. Our son attended elementary school just up the road from our home. We got him and our daughter up, fed and dressed. We always walked him to school and picked him up after. (We lived too close for bus services.)

This day was especially warm and sunny for September. Our son, backpack on his back, packed and ready to go, was as excited for his day as he always was. He loved school. Our daughter, tucked neatly into her stroller, ready for our morning trek to school. As we walked, my wife and I talked about many different things while our son led the way and our daughter giggled and rode in style. We arrived at the school without incident. A quick kiss and hug for us all and he was inside, ready to start his day. As we walked back home, taking our time and enjoying the beautiful weather, we again talked about various topics.

Once home, I took our daughter inside, sat her on the living room floor and switched on the TV. What I saw shocked me, as I'm sure it shocked the rest of the world. The World Trade Center was ablaze. I called my wife into the room and showed her. Panic set in. Both her brother and his wife worked in the Trade Centers. As she frantically attempted to get ahold of him, I found myself unable to stop watching the tragedy unfolding in front of me on live TV. My first thought was about my brothers and sisters of the FDNY, before I was reminded that my brother-in-law worked there. I was worried for their safety. As I watched live on CNN, the other tower exploded into a fireball. I remember a few expletives leaving my lips and without thinking, I told my wife the other tower just blew up. She came in to see. With total fear on her face, she told me she was unable, so far, to contact her brother. My heart sank. I remember pleading with God to please help her hear from her brother and to please keep him safe. The replay that CNN showed next was just prior to the second tower being involved. It showed a large aircraft swoop down and crash right into the building. I remember thinking, "We're being attacked by our own planes!" Why were they doing this? I would learn the truth much later.

My wife was talking to someone on the phone at this point. She came back to where I was standing and told me she was able to contact her brother. He was safe. Thank God! He had not left for work yet and was watching it on TV just as we were, however, his wife had left for work and should already be in the tower by now. Panic and worry set in big time. He said he would call as soon as he knew she was safe. We sat there watching all the events unfold. CNN had reporters on the streets below the towers and were constantly updating the world on the events while stopping random people asking them what they saw. They saw a plane hit the freaking building, you idiot, were my thoughts as they interviewed visibly shaken civilians. Video of fire engines, rescue trucks, ambulances and police cars flooded the television. Firefighters in full turnout gear, wearing SCBAs (self-contained breathing apparatus'), carrying tools, hoses and spare bottles walking towards the chaos, as others ran for their lives. I didn't envy the task ahead of them but I admired their bravery. I'm sure they were as scared as we all were, walking into the unknown.

I don't remember the time frame that followed but my brother-in-law called back to let us know his wife was safe. She was coming up from the subway just as the second tower was struck. She promptly found a taxi and went home. They were both safe, we were relieved.

Now the news shifted to the Pentagon in Washington, telling of an explosion and fire there. What the hell was going on, I thought. Now I knew we were under attack! They showed video from Washington, one side of the building was billowing smoke and flames. I felt helpless just watching. Instinct told me I needed to do something, but what?

I watched. Newscasters speculated, contacted terrorism experts who ventured their best guesses as to why this is happening and who's responsible. Nobody knew at the time, they were just guessing. Rumors circulated about other planes being hijacked and potential targets. The White House and Capitol buildings were evacuated as precautions. Back to New York. Both towers were burning heavily now. I knew what was happening in the command post there. Teams were being identified and given assignments. Ascend the stairs of 1 and 2 World Trade and do whatever you can. Make rescues if possible, assist in evacuating survivors and fight whatever fire you can. Report back on what resources you need. Now, picture this, each firefighter carries 65 pounds of turnout gear on their bodies including SCBAs on their backs. They carry pry bars, axes and other various tools. They also bring hose with them to attach to water outlets in the stairwells, also known as "stand pipes," to fight the fire. They had to carry these items up 89 flights and when they got to the fire, attach the hoses and spray water on the fire, all while looking for survivors. This is a very demanding job, both physically and emotionally. Along the way, they were met by a stampede of people trying to escape.

Time seemed to stand still, then it happened. Tower 2, the second one hit, disappeared into a cloud of smoke and dust. I remember sitting there holding my breath, hoping all got out of the building prior to this. All I could say was, "Oh my God," over and over again. My heart hurt. I knew firefighters were inside. I prayed for their safety. A short time later, Tower 1 also collapsed. I shook inside. This was a tremendous tragedy, for not only the fire service, but for America. I remember feeling like I needed to be there, to help out.

I should have been in bed hours ago. I had to work at 9 p.m. that night. There was no way I could sleep after what I witnessed. What I do remember after all that was the ride to work, seeing a couple of local fire department service vehicles, lights flashing, New York bound. Once I was at work, I contacted our union president and asked if we were sending anyone down. He told me the mayor wouldn't authorize it. I was pissed! Our brothers and sisters needed help and I couldn't go. I walked outside and looked up at the stars. The president had grounded all aircraft. It was the first time the skies were free of anything but stars. It was also eerily quiet.

It wasn't until much later that I would find out just how large the loss of life was. Firefighters, EMS personnel, police, FBI, ATF and civilians. Some FDNY companies lost entire platoon shifts as well as equipment. The numbers were staggering. For days and weeks after, rescue missions turned into recovery missions. It was a very sad time for public safety as well as the world.

Not All Calls Are Routine

Over the next few weeks, I had gone to multiple therapy sessions. This therapist was a godsend! She started digging into my past, pulling out things I had long forgotten. Things from my childhood and beyond. I don't really remember which one it was, but during one session she stopped me, looked at me and said I had PTSD. She believes it started early on in my life and progressively got worse, starting with my very first fatal accident. Back then, we didn't discuss our feelings in the firehouse. You were expected to be strong, shrug it off and move on. So all the carnage I saw and was involved in over the years had built up inside of me to a point where Chip's death was the final blow. She called it the "cup half full scenario." Normally used for optimism vs. pessimism, this was used as a way to describe a coping skill for people with PTSD. As we encounter trauma, our psychological glasses fill. How we deal with it determines whether our glass empties or remains full. Since I never really dealt with anything I saw, my glass overflowed to the point where dealing with anything new was not an option anymore. There was no more room. I needed to empty the glass and that was what she was trying to do.

She abandoned the past and started me with things in the present, figuring to work backwards since it was fresh. We talked at length about Chip, my actions, my reactions, my feelings and how to deal with it. This went on for a couple of sessions, getting me to the point where the nightmares finally stopped and I was sleeping again, but it didn't end there. I was still working and the calls were still coming, adding to things I had to deal with. One call would prove to be very challenging.

I was working my night shift, 9 p.m. to 7 a.m. Around 1 or 2 in the morning, I received a call for a person with difficulty breathing. There were no volunteers in the firehouse this night so I left in the ambulance alone. I arrived on scene to find a semi-conscious female on her front steps surrounded by family members. I got out of the ambulance, opened the compartment containing my med bag, and started for the steps. Two males, who I found out later were her sons, picked her up and started walking her toward me. I asked them to put her down so I could examine her and was met with anger. They opened the back doors of my ambulance and lifted her up and on to my stretcher. I informed them that I was by myself and needed to wait for my partner to arrive before we could transport her. At this point I was surrounded by 7 people who told me I was to treat her or they would do me bodily harm (being polite with not using their exact wording). One of the males told me to get in and he'd drive me to the hospital. I immediately got on my portable and requested police assistance ASAP (as soon as possible), translated into FD lingo meant RIGHT NOW! I stood there trying to explain to these people that things didn't work like that, to which they reiterated their intentions. At this point I felt two hands on my shoulders. I spun around to find the volunteer fire captain standing behind me.

He said, "Get in and hang on!" I jumped into the back of the ambulance and strapped my patient onto the stretcher. He closed the doors, got in the driver's seat and drove us out of there. We stopped in the elementary school parking lot a couple of blocks away. He got out and came into the back with me to assist. I was never so happy to see anyone as I was him that night. We stabilized my patient and he drove us to the hospital. Once the patient was safely in the hospital, I informed the staff of the interaction I had with the family. They immediately contacted hospital security and made them aware. We left the hospital and proceeded back to the firehouse with me thanking him the whole way. This man has been a good friend for years but this night, he was my knight in shining armor. I don't care how that sounds. He saved me from getting my ass kicked.

Telling my therapist about this was as comical as it was scary. I was the most scared I'd been in a long time. I was also very angry that they did that to me. I tried to reason it away with things like, they were upset, they were scared. Turns out, they were just drunk jerks! She helped me process it and put it away. If I didn't have her, who knows where I would have been, mentally, after that incident. My glass wasn't empty yet. Hell, it wasn't even a quarter of the way down.

She told me I needed a vacation from all this for a while, a chance to reboot if you will. I agreed. I loved my job but I was still afraid that if I did leave, even for a vacation, I would never return. My job gives me four weeks of vacation each year, what better reason to use it. I spent a couple of weeks away from work trying to enjoy my family. Therapy continued through my vacation. The time away was nice and going back, I felt refreshed and ready to take on the world. I didn't know it then, but I was far from ready.

Defining My Logic

I can only speak for myself when it comes to PTSD. I see myself as "labeled" with something that makes me different. I'm not different. I'm the same person I've been all my life, I've just seen more horrific things than most people, things that would give "normal" people nightmares for the rest of their life. No, I'm not different; I'm a survivor!

Webster defines "disorder" as a state in which everything is out of order. The medical definition is: "to disturb the regular or normal function of." To say that my normal function has been disturbed is an understatement. Things that are easy for most are hard for me at times, like grocery shopping. Large crowds make me nervous and anxious, not all the time but if I'm having a bad day, forget it! Tying my shoes. If the loop doesn't stay on the first shot, my shoe comes off and goes across the room. Simple things aren't so simple anymore but they will be again. Therapy has gotten me to a place where grocery shopping isn't a task and my shoes stay on my feet where they belong.

If you know of someone or hear of somebody who has PTSD please treat them as you would any other person. Just keep in the back of your mind that they have this disorder and remember to always be gentle when necessary. Never ask someone with PTSD how they got it. If they bring it up, please listen to them. The best thing for us is to talk about how it makes us feel, not so much what caused it but how we are and how we are doing coping with it.

PTSD doesn't have to be a death sentence. It is a fact of life for many first responders and military members who fought in wars. It's a fact of life for me. I'll have PTSD for the rest of my life. I've finally accepted that fact. I refuse to allow it to run my life though, this is why I'm in therapy. The other problem is, I love my job. To me, it's not a job but a calling. As I said before, I didn't choose the Fire Service, it chose me! As I continue to respond to calls, I find that I ask myself, "When will it be too much?" My answer? It'll never be too much. I see no end in site and I'm ok with that.

One thing I'll say again is, please, don't ever ask a firefighter, EMS provider, police officer or military member, "What's the worst thing you've ever seen?" You're asking them to relive a terror or horrific scene that they probably don't want to think about. Besides, you probably don't want to know anyway. I don't like sharing my nightmares. Why would you want them! Some of the calls I've encountered involve children, young adults, grown adults, elderly and of course babies. I've assisted in two deliveries (well, I say assisted, as I walked through the door the babies had just been born). There is suctioning that needs to be done and evaluations on both baby and mom. For all the death I've seen, these two events make up for a lot of it.

I've been called crazy, stupid, brave and "out of my mind" for doing what I do and the crap that comes along with it. You almost have to be a little touched in the head to do this job. How many sane people run *in* a burning building when everyone else is running out.

How many sane people will search an accident site for a severed limb in hopes of finding it and bringing it to the hospital for reattachment. Every one of us! Speaking for myself, I do this job because I enjoy helping. I have always felt I could make a difference. Sometimes I do. Other times, it doesn't matter what you do, the outcome isn't favorable. I understand we can't save everyone, but from someone with PTSD, the ones who don't survive haunt me for days after. Did I do everything I could, did I do everything right, etc. Sometimes I blame myself, sometimes I blame God. Why did He help me obtain this skill and knowledge only to have me fail? It's hard sometimes to accept the fact that people die. That it's the natural course of life. In time, my brain will be retaught how to accept fate, but for now, I'm not able.

On many occasions, I find myself sitting alone and thinking. Some days it's a good thing, others, not so much. Unfortunately for me, PTSD brain is like a VCR stuck on rewind. I replay my calls over and over in my mind, and not the good calls. Why can't it be the good calls? The other side of this is when I'm thinking of these calls, other bad calls jumps on the bandwagon and come along also. It's kind of like a double whammy! My therapist says I'll remember and process things when my brain feels I'm ready. The longer I'm in therapy, the more these things will happen. Thankfully I have a great therapist, wonderful family and supportive friends. These are all things anyone who has PTSD needs.

The Day I Lost A Part of Me

Things seemed to be happening to me, health-wise, as I started deeper into therapy. The first thing to go was my appendix. It started at 6 a.m. as a cramping in my stomach. I figured it was what I ate the night before. The odd thing about it was it came in waves, each one progressively worse than the one before. Now I've transported many people with acute appendicitis and they have always had pain in the lower right quadrant of the abdomen with a slight fever, sweating and vomiting. My pains were center of my abdomen, above my belly button, no sweating and no vomiting. My wife ran to the store to get me some antacids in hopes that it would cure this pain I felt. After a couple of hours of this I couldn't take it anymore and asked her to drive me to the hospital.

They placed me in a room fairly quickly and started their evaluation. Blood was drawn and x-rays were ordered. While waiting for the bloodwork to come back, I was taken to x-ray. The technician asked me to lay flat on my back. When I did this I felt a tremendous pulling and pain in my stomach. I told him laying flat wasn't going to happen. He tried insisting on it but when a person with PTSD says he isn't doing something, you have a better chance getting that horse to drink that you just led to water! Needless to say we improvised and we both got our way, him his x-ray and me not lying flat.

I was returned to my treatment room where a nurse came in and handed me a bucket. I told her I wasn't feeling nauseous. She smiled and walked away. The doctor came into the room and informed me that my bloodwork came back and my white cell count was not just elevated but through the roof. His diagnosis, appendicitis! I told him I wasn't having any of the classic symptoms but he informed me that a surgeon would be coming in to evaluate me. At this point is when I vomited for the first time. I was starting to second guess myself. An IV tech came in and started a 1000 bag of saline. The nurse was close behind with anti-nausea meds. Soon, a woman dressed in scrubs came into my room, introduced herself to me, asked me some brief questions and told me to lay back. As soon as she touched my lower right side, I about launched off the bed and immediately started vomiting again. She confirmed the ER doctor's diagnosis, said she'd see me upstairs soon, waved to us and out the door she went.

At this point, I just wanted to go home. I hate hospitals! After a short stay in the ER, I was taken upstairs to a private room, my wife close by my side, our son with a babysitter. My nurse upstairs informed us that as soon as a surgical suite came available I would be going. It was now early to mid-afternoon. The anti-nausea meds were working well and they had also given me some pain meds. I remember some friends coming to visit me. Around 7 p.m. or 8, my wife said she was headed home to put our son to bed and she'd be right back. After she left, I remember lying there feeling scared. I'd had surgeries before but none I didn't prepare for.

I don't think my wife was gone 10 minutes when the nurse came in with two pills she asked me to take. She informed me that a surgical suite had come open and they would be coming to take me in a few minutes. Now I was really scared. I asked her to please call my wife and inform her I was going to surgery. Soon after, two people dressed in surgical attire arrived and transferred me from my bed to another.

When I arrived on the surgical floor, I was met by a doctor who introduced himself to me. He examined me by pressing on my abdomen in many places. Thanks to the wonderful pain meds, I not only didn't feel this but I could lie flat. When he was done, he bent down close to me and told me it was my lucky day, he was having a two for one special. It appeared I also had a hernia that I didn't know about. Go figure!

Then I asked the million dollar question, will I be catheterized? He told me I would. Now, I'm not ashamed to admit that I'm a big ole baby when it comes to some things. This was one of the biggies! I asked him to please wait until I was under before doing that and to please insure it came out before I woke up. He smiled and reassured me that my wishes would be met.

They wheeled me into this large room. I remember music playing in the background and lots of people dressed in scrubs with masks on. They gently transferred me from my bed to the surgical table. A guy at my head asked me my name, asked if I was allergic to any meds and calmed me. I watched as he inserted a syringe into my IV tube. Once he had pushed all the medication in, he asked me to start counting backwards from 10. I asked him why I wasn't counting back from 100 since that's how it's done on TV. I don't remember anything else after that until I woke up in recovery.

As I came back to reality in recovery, I felt a tug and realized they were removing my catheter. Wow, what a wake up! I opened my eyes as the nurse was pulling the cover back up over me. I ask her how it went. She informed me that the doctor was speaking with my wife and would be in shortly to talk to me. I had dozed off for a few when the doctor came in. He said my hernia was an easy fix. He just had to push my intestine back through the abdominal muscle. My appendix, however, was another story. He informed me that the surgery was done laparoscopically. He said he made a small incision just below my belly button, injected air into my abdomen to inflate it, and inserted a small device to do the job. The problem was, my appendix was tangled in my intestines and it was huge! He had to make two other incisions to get at it. Once he had a hold of it, he removed it from mead. He had it in his hands over the specimen tray when it burst open. Lucky for me, it wasn't in there any later or it would have burst inside of me. He told me he placed what was left in the specimen tray, applied fresh gloves and closed me up. I asked about my wife. He told me that he'd met with her already, filled her in on everything, told her I'd be in recovery for a little while and that I'd see her when I got back to my room. He informed me he would be back in the morning to see me, shook my hand and left. I was relieved it was over, more relieved that the catheter was out of me!

I woke up as we were getting back to my room. I remember seeing my wife there, concern quickly leaving her face when I smiled at her. They helped me into my bed, covered me up and told my wife that if I needed anything to just hit the call button. I'm sure I spoke to my wife but I just don't remember. I woke the next morning to find her asleep in a rollout bed next to mine. This was my support system.

The doctor came in later in the morning, explained everything to me again, and asked how I was. My stomach was twice its normal size and I was concerned about that. He told me it would reduce naturally. He said he wanted me up and out of bed as soon as I was able. He told me to walk as much as I could but not to push myself too much, too soon. We both thanked him and he was gone.

The first day, I was up and walking. I was able to make one lap around the nurses station. As time went on, I got better and better. The second day, the doctor came in, examined me and said he wanted me to stay one more day. The last day, I felt great. My stomach still looked like I was pregnant but physically, I felt good. When my wife came to get me, she had a pair of sweatpants and a clean shirt. It felt good to get out of the hospital gown. I was sent home to finish my recovery, which I did in record time. My stomach eventually went back to normal and in a couple of weeks I was cleared to go back to work. This, I would learn later, was just the start of my health issues.

Ice Rescue

The winter of 2007 was a particularly cold one. We had many days where the temperature didn't come up above freezing. This one shift I would have a couple of firsts in my career.

I was working my regular 25 hour shift when I received a phone call at the station. A woman who lived on the lake in town was reporting two dogs that had fallen through the ice and couldn't get out. She asked if we would help them. I took all her information and told her we would figure something out. The fire chief happened to be at the station at this time, so I relayed all the information she had given me and asked him how he wanted to handle it. He told me to contact dispatch and have it put out as an ice rescue. I did this and went to our company service truck to retrieve our boat, a small Zodiac inflatable, in case we needed it. I also grabbed our cold water rescue suits and rope.

This particular lake was bordered by two other towns. When there was an emergency all those towns were also dispatched. This lake is a popular venue for ice fishing in the winter and local residents also liked to walk on the ice. This year, the ice was very thick in spots but it did have its weak areas. Apparently these two dogs had found one of those areas.

The fire chief was first to arrive at the location and quickly updated us on the status of the dogs. He stated they were about 500-1000 feet from shore and could clearly see they were struggling.

He asked my location and requested I expedite to the scene.

I arrived and quickly made contact with the chief. He showed me, through binoculars, the exact location of the dogs. It was going to be quite a hike to get to them. I went back to my truck, removed one of the cold water suits and quickly got dressed. At this time, other resources from the area departments started to arrive. When I got down to the shore, we developed a game plan of getting onto the ice, how many rescuers were going and who was shore support. During any ice rescue, you need a support team on shore. All rescuers are dressed in suits that are pretty much airtight. These are like divers wet suits, just bigger. We are attached to rescue rope, in case we fall in or to pull us back once the rescue is complete. This is definitely not a one man operation. Just before heading out onto the ice I heard a helicopter overhead. The local news station was returning to their home station after having routine maintenance done and were almost over the location when the call came in. I remember looking up and saying to myself, "Great, news crews! Don't screw up or you'll be all over the news."

I was accompanied by two other firefighters, one had a ice sled which is designed to move over the ice with ease or float like a boat if the ice breaks. We moved very slowly at first, testing the ice as we went. We needed to keep quite a bit of distance between us, if the ice broke under one of us then only one would go in the water and not the whole team. It seemed to take forever to reach the dogs. I also remember wishing the helicopter would drop a rope and tow us to the dogs. Too Hollywood, I thought.

I could see the dogs more clearly now. We were within 100 feet of them. The one rescuer with us reached the end of his lifeline and had to hold, leaving myself and the other rescuer with the ice sled to continue. I was so focused on the goal of reaching the dogs that I wasn't paying attention to what was under me. I found a weak area of ice and down I went. Thankfully these suits are designed as one big flotation device. As soon as I hit the water, the suit gripped around my legs and my upper body swelled up like the Michelin Man. I put my arms out like an airplane and caught myself on the ice. I'm now shoulder deep in the water. One strong bob and I was able to pop right out and back onto solid ice. Without missing a beat, I pressed on. On my hands and knees crawling, having learned my lesson, I crawled toward the hole where the dogs were. Those two were struggling real hard now. I crawled faster till I reached the hole. I had a pole with a rope loop on it. I extended the pole and put the loop over one of the dogs head. He and I were now face to face. I can't explain it, but he looked at me like, "Come on dude, get me outta here!" I reached down, grabbed his collar and with one strong yank, he was out. I passed him off to the other rescuer and went after number two. This one actually swam to me. I reached in, grabbed his collar and with a couple of pulls, he was out. This one was so happy to be out that he tried to run to shore. I grabbed on to him, sat him and myself on the ice sled, gave the signal and the shore team pulled us to safety.

Once on shore, the team quickly wrapped the dogs in blankets and carried them to the waiting ambulance. There they were warmed and given water. After a series of handshakes, high fives and fist bumps, I just wanted out of the suit. I went back to my truck, removed the suit and placed it on to the rear seat. I walked over to the ambulance to check on the dogs and found them to be well cared for. After a quick debriefing we all departed, the dogs turned over to the owner for a trip to the vet for evaluation.

Arriving back at the station, I placed my cold water suit in the rear garage where it would hang to dry. Walking back into the main building I was met by the fire chief. He informed me that the news station had called and wanted to do an interview with me. I told him I didn't think I could. We have a policy that forbids the career staff from talking to the media. He said he cleared it with my boss and I was to do the interview. Wonderful! (Stated sarcastically!)

Later that afternoon a female reporter from the news station arrived. I introduced myself to her. She asked me basic questions about the rescue and my experience. She then told me how everyone at the station watched the rescue from the helicopter's live feed as it happened. When the second dog was removed, everyone clapped and cheered. That made me feel really good.

We filmed the interview in front of the ambulance. My story ran on the 6 and 11 o'clock news. It wasn't until the next day and the phone calls started that I found out my story went national. CNN, *Inside Edition*, The Weather Channel and others were running the story. I didn't know what to say. I'd never had this much notoriety. It was my very first ice rescue and my very first television interview. I guess I can call this my 15 minutes of fame.

One For The Books

People I know, who are not in the fire service, have asked me why I keep doing this job if it bothers me. The job doesn't bother me. Some of the calls I go on do, but it's the nature of the beast. They say, "Why not just quit and do something else?" Okay. Why don't you just stop breathing, stop eating and stop living! This job is all I know. This career field picked me! I don't want to stop; I love what I do.

Having PTSD has taught me that with the good side of this job comes the bad also. As in life, we have good days and bad days. I've learned how to process everything. Whereas before, I pushed all the bad down inside my brain, filling it to capacity until the top blew off and when it did, it changed my life and the lives of everyone I love.

After 37 years of doing this job, I've come in contact with many people who are having their worst possible day. I've included a lot of those in this book. Some I have not included because I just don't remember for whatever reason. The ones I have included stick in my memory, either I'm still processing them or they've left a permanent mark on me. This one I'm about to share has definitely left a scar. I know I'm still processing this one. I've seen many things in this job but this one was something that left me cold.

Working my regular shift—I believe it was a Friday night—I received a call for a one car motor vehicle accident (MVA) versus a tree. I went into the bays, put on my gear and got into the engine. As I was headed to the scene, dispatch advised reports were coming in for serious injuries. I remember there being a very fine misty fog over the area this night, not unusual for a summer evening. As I arrived, I was shocked at what I saw. The accident happened on a moderate curve. I found a truck, a Chevy I believe, with a utility body on it. The truck had hit a tree almost center of the vehicle. They hit this tree with so much force that the tree penetrated the truck, split the driver and passenger seats and stopped at the front of the utility body. As I exited the engine, the first thing I saw was the cab of the truck suspended in the air (front wheels off the ground). The cab of the truck was actually hugging the tree. I looked into the passenger window and saw a person, turned slightly with his back against the door and window. I could see he was moving.

What I witnessed next would shock me. There was a civilian in the back of the truck yelling for me to hurry. I approached the side of the vehicle, placed my foot on the right rear tire and gently pulled myself up.

What I saw next was death waiting to happen. The force of the impact had shoved the driver through the rear window into the utility body of the truck. He was pinned from the waist down in the cab. Lying on his back, eyes wide open and gasping for air, he moved his head slowly from side to side. I tried to look inside the cab, from my vantage point, to see how badly he was pinned. The dashboard was pressed up against his abdomen. There was approximately 1-2 inches between the dashboard and the back wall of the cab. I knew at this point he would be a difficult extrication. I looked back at my patient. He had stopped moving, eyes still wide open, he gasped two more times, slow and drawn, then stopped. This man had expired right in front of me and there wasn't a damn thing I could do about it. I looked at the individual with him, asked him if he was involved in the crash and told him to get out of the truck. He said he didn't want to leave the man. I informed him the person was deceased and he needed to get out, the truck wasn't stable.

I needed much more help with this call so I got on the radio, requested another heavy rescue, a second ambulance and the helicopter. Soon after this the fire chief arrived and I briefed him on the status of the incident. He took over as command and I went to work getting the Jaws of Life and other equipment out and ready to use. Other resources soon arrived and we went to work getting the passenger extricated. He must have had his arm across the top of the seat at impact because the majority of his pin was the tree pinning his arm against the back of the truck. This extrication would prove to be very tricky. The cab was suspended off the ground a good 4 feet and crews were having a hard time getting their footing and stabilizing the truck. A heavy duty wrecker was brought in to assist. They attached a cable to the right rear of the truck and pulled it slightly off the tree to complete the extrication.

The helicopter was unable to fly due to weather so the passenger was transported to the trauma center by ambulance with a paramedic riding along. Now came the task of picking up equipment and waiting for the State Police Accident Reconstruction Team, as well as the Medical Examiner. Now, anyone in this field knows this is a time consuming process. Measurements must be taken, photos of the scene and interviews of witnesses. While this was going on, I walked around the truck to see the scene full on. I couldn't imagine how fast they had to be going to do this much damage.

The M.E. arrived just as the state police were finishing up their process. Now came the difficult task of removing the driver. Many ideas were discussed and shot down. The one that seemed most logical was to have the wrecker driver pull the truck away from the tree. As this happened, the M.E. retrieved his equipment. Slowly the wrecker pulled. I don't think anyone expected what happened next. The cab and body of the truck reached their breaking points and separated. As this happened, the driver was released from the grip of the truck. A few of us assisted the M.E. with his examination and movement of the body. What I couldn't see from my vantage point earlier was the driver had been cut in half just above his pelvis. The pressure from the position slowed his bleeding causing him to expire slowly. We helped get the driver into the M.E. van for transport to Farmington. Nobody said a word as we worked together getting the rest of the equipment back onto the engine. The scene was finally cleared and we returned to the station.

Driving back to the fire department, I was watching the sunrise through the windshield and thinking about the family members waking this morning to the horrible news of last night's accident. Some would be going to a hospital to comfort loved ones and support the man injured and some would be grieving. I felt sad for those people. I felt like I'd let them down by not doing more, even though I knew there was nothing at all humanly possible that could have been done. I wanted to cry.

As I backed the engine into the station, I couldn't get those two guys out of my head. I got angry now. How dare they make me go through that, see what I saw! I can't ever unsee that. What the hell was wrong with them, damn them! That wasn't me, that was the PTSD. My brain was reacting to this event and processing what it could for the time being. I wasn't handling this well at all.

I saw my therapist soon after this call and poured my heart out. I cried, I was angry, I felt remorse and about a hundred different emotions all at the same time. This is what PTSD has done to me.

On a good note, it has also helped me get in touch with a side of me I'd lost contact with years ago. It's made me a better person that way. I still think about those two from time to time, unfortunately, I pass the location of that accident on many occasions so it's a constant reminder. That's not a bad thing. Sometimes we need to be reminded of things that bothered us so we can properly deal with the ramifications of those events. It's helped me anyway.

Facing Reality

It took me a long time to admit I had PTSD. I was embarrassed and ashamed. I felt weak. I figured my friends and fellow firefighters would look down on me as being a "drama queen". This only fueled my symptoms. I was feeling unsure of myself and my abilities, both as a firefighter/EMT and as a human being. What I didn't understand, at that moment, was that PTSD had a firm hold of my emotions. Crowds scared me. They made me feel anxiety like I'd never felt before, therefore, I never wanted to go anywhere.

The emotions associated with PTSD are nothing more than a vicious circle. There were times I felt good about myself, then I felt guilty for feeling good — like I didn't deserve it. I wouldn't buy things for myself, I didn't feel like I deserved it. I wouldn't buy foods I liked because I didn't feel like I deserved it. Seeing the pattern yet? PTSD took over my self worth and dumped it into the crapper! Feeling this way only made me more frustrated and angry. Even during therapy I wouldn't speak up 100% about how I was feeling. I didn't think I deserved the help. My therapist, being the amazing individual she is, saw through this and pushed and pulled until it came out, reducing me to a emotional blob.

Some of the things I still battle to this day are emotional roller coasters. They come out of nowhere. One minute I'm going along with my day and something will trigger me, set me off and now I'm crying uncontrollably. These things blindside me from time to time.

The problem is, I never know when they'll hit or for how long. Writing this book had caused triggers. Of course it has, I'm reliving every horrific call I've had since 1977, what did I think would happen! I wrote the chapter about the MVA with the truck that was split down the middle. After, I made a trip to the store to replenish my supply of Gatorade. I walked in, looked around and saw a large amount of people in the store. As I made my way to the back aisles I found myself starting to shake, my heart started racing and I couldn't breathe. I was having a panic attack. I hadn't had one like this in years, why now? I turned and left the store as quickly as I could. I sat in my Jeep, breathed deeply, told myself I was safe and was able to relax. Once I was better, I exited my Jeep and went back into the store. I went directly to the aisle I needed, got what I came for and went directly to the self checkout (no lines and I could go quick). Once I paid, I grabbed my stuff and ran out. It took the rest of the day, and my families support, to relax. After I calmed down completely, my body felt like I had just ran a marathon; my muscles were very sore and I was physically exhausted. This is common after one of my panic attacks.

Even now, seeing this on paper knowing all my friends and family are going to read this is kind of embarrassing. In my mind you are all judging me as weak. I know it's not true. PTSD is nothing to be ashamed of. I didn't ask for this. I have it because I cared, because I helped and because I chose to volunteer and eventually work in a field that takes a special kind of crazy to do.

PTSD is not curable but it is manageable with the right therapy and support. Family, friends and coworkers are key figures in keeping those of us with this disease alive and well. Yes, I said alive. Too often, someone with PTSD takes their own life due to the demons running rampant in their mind. Thankfully, my demons are caged and under control. Every once in a while, one of those little bastards escapes and starts causing problems. That's where my family, friends and therapist come in to corral him and lock him away where he belongs. I'll have this for the rest of my life but I'm living proof that it can be managed and it can be overcome.

One other side of PTSD is uncontrollable anger, either at myself or others. This is usually accompanied by frustration. I'll feel the anger, try to control it, fail and get frustrated. I've been taught to examine why I'm angry, if it's valid and how I can overcome it. It's hard, trust me. It's very difficult sometimes and I'm an impatient person when it comes to negative emotions, I don't have time for them. I've learned, and am still learning everyday, how to calm myself first then go after what's causing the anger. This is still a work in progress.

When I first started in the fire service, dark humor was a great cover for grief. It was also the accepted practice among firefighters: don't show emotion, it's a sign of weakness. My answer to that, ppffftttt! I'm a human being doing a difficult, thankless job and I'm going to get emotionally involved in all the serious calls I go to. I'm not a robot, I can't pick and choose which ones will affect me and which ones won't. It doesn't work that way and the sooner people realize this fact the better off we'll all be. Maybe then help will be even more readily available.

I have PTSD and it's not the end of the world or the end of my life!

Self Healing

In 37 years of doing this, I've responded to many incidents. Some I've included in this book, mainly to show how and why I was diagnosed with PTSD. Many calls I have not written about because if I remembered them all, this book would be as thick as *War and Peace*, but also, there are incidents I refuse to write about: suicides. I've seen and been involved with way more than I needed to. I refuse to write about them or detail them out of respect to the families and the individuals themselves.

Suicide causes so much pain on so many levels. Not just the the individual whose demons took over and consumed them so much that they felt they had no choice but to end their life, but also the families and friends left behind to try and make sense of all of it. Being a EMT, it's our job to respond to these incidents, examine the victim for signs of life and provide care if possible. If no care is possible, now we turn our attention to the family present who witnessed this event, insure their well being, say some consoling words and leave. It doesn't end there, at least not for me. I carry it for a while. I wonder what was so wrong in someone's life that they felt they needed to take such drastic measures to end their pain. Problems are temporary; death is permanent!

The suicide rate among first responders is growing daily. Many times the victims had PTSD and never sought help or reached out. Sometimes we can't reach out, the pain is too much. It's up to the rest of us to look out for our brothers and sisters. We see some of them as much as their families do so we know their demeanors. Look for obvious changes in their personalities. Sometimes the changes aren't so obvious, but they're still changes. Changes in eating habits, sleeping habits and sociability. These are all warning signs. It's best to catch it early. Don't confront them, you'll only put them on the defensive. Ask questions about them or their family. You can find out so much just through casual conversation.

If they break down, comfort them. I know when I was first diagnosed and would have emotional breakdowns, I didn't want to be touched. I wanted to be left alone. Sometimes this was good for me to evaluate myself, sometimes this was bad because I would turn on myself and start into a downward spiral. Emotions depend on the individual, there's no textbook answer to any of this. The best friend one can have is one who listens intently, comforts honestly and is always available in time of crisis.

There are times I had to self medicate. What I mean by that is, when I started having a bad day, either anger or depression, I turned to TV. Cartoons were the best thing I found to bring me out of any sadness or depression. My favorite was Bugs Bunny. I grew up with Bugs, he and I spent many Saturday mornings sharing a bowl of cereal together. I always felt better after watching cartoons. My therapist says it's because it brings me back to my childhood, no pressures and no responsibilities. I didn't care why, it worked and that made me happy. When Bugs wasn't on TV, I walked alone and thought about what was causing my grief. Sometimes I figured it out, other times I needed help with it. When walking wasn't going to work, my last resort was Playstation. Video games were a great outlet for frustration. I could kill as many people and things as I wanted and still be free from prosecution.

My therapy and support system helped get me to a place where I could deal with whatever life threw at me. Sometimes I had minor setback but, for the most part, I was a productive member of society again. That would be tested in a big way on September 4, 2012. That's the day my Mom died.

Mom

My parents moved to Florida in 1995 after my dad fully retired. They had found a wonderful retirement community on the west coast. We traveled many times to go and visit them. It was a great getaway for us and my parents got to spoil their grandchildren.

Early in 2012 I received a phone call from my dad saying my mom had fallen. She fell often and usually required a response from the local fire department to assist her to her feet. Once she was up she was fine, usually. This time she couldn't stand on her own so the ambulance transported her to a local hospital for evaluation. My dad seemed optimistic that Mom would be fine and return home soon. I asked him to keep me updated. He called many times to inform me on her progress and gave me her number so I could speak to her also. When we talked on the phone, she sounded depressed. She just wanted to go home. I could understand her not wanting to be there, I don't care much for hospitals either.

A couple of days went by and my dad informed me they were moving my mom to a rehab facility for physical therapy. Her legs had lost strength and they needed to find out why and rebuild her muscle tone. She was moved to facility that was quite a distance from my parent's home but my dad never missed a day seeing my mom.

I don't exactly remember the timeline of events from this point on. Either I blocked them out or it's just too hard for my brain to handle yet but I'll do my best.

My mom had an MRI on her spine and the doctor found that her spinal cord was degenerating and it was affecting all the nerve endings. Her mental status started to be affected soon after this and her memory was the first to feel the brunt. My dad and the doctor worked together to get my mom moved to facility closer to their home so my dad didn't have to drive so far and so her friends could visit.

This went on for weeks, my mom questioning my dad on when she could go home, even though she'd been told on numerous occasions that she would not ever be going home again. I would call her and I noticed changes in her. She sounded tired, she'd repeat questions and would call me by my other brother's names. Then the big blow. My dad called and said eventually this degeneration would reach her brain. It was progressing at a rapid rate and the doctor was giving my mother months to live. I was devastated. My mom and I didn't always have the best relationship but she was my mommy and I loved her. The phone calls slowed down over the next few weeks, mainly due to my mom's mental status. She would be sleeping a lot or would talk for a short time then ask to go.

During this time my wife, kids and I did what we needed to do to try and not think about any of this, it was just too hard. We spent a lot of time going to the park, out to dinner and just being good to ourselves. The one thing I didn't count on was my PTSD coming back full force. I didn't have time for this!

September 4, 2012 started just as any other day did. We went about our business together. We had been out shopping, I think. I know we had just gotten home around 11 a.m. or 12 when my phone rang. I looked at the caller ID, Dad. My heart sank. I answered the phone and spoke quietly. Honestly, the only thing I remember is my dad saying, "Your mom closed her eyes and went to sleep. She's at peace now." I burst into tears! My family ran to me and wrapped their arms around me and we cried uncontrollably. My dad asked if we were ok. I assured him we would be, said I loved him and hung up. He had to make other phone calls to notify other family members.

I sat down on the couch and cried. My mom was gone. I never got the chance to say goodbye or hug her just one more time. I felt lost. Even now, I'm crying as I write this. I loved my mom and I miss her so much.

I called out of work and surrounded myself with my wife and kids. We clung to each other for the next few days. We were never far apart and they wouldn't let me get far without one of them by my side. This helped tremendously and I can't ever thank them enough for loving me the way they did throughout all this.

My mom was to be cremated, per her wishes. There was no funeral in Florida for her. My dad had arranged a memorial service to be held in February once all the residents had returned from their summer vacations. My brother and I arranged a memorial service here for us and her friends who were still here. I asked for use of the hall at the fire department I'm assigned to. It was given to me free of charge. We arranged for a meal to be catered and sent out the invitations in the paper.

It was more of a gathering than a memorial service. Friends of both my mom and dad, as well as my friends and family came and enjoyed stories of my mom and how she touched other's lives. We all hugged, laughed and cried. When it was over, our lives needed to continue on. Mine would take a turn that I didn't expect. PTSD was back and in full force.

Epilogue

PTSD came back for me in a big way. Anger, depression, mood swings and feelings of poor self worth. I didn't notice any of this right away. My wife would ask me how I was doing and I would say, "okay," and leave it at that. I was far from okay!

I had stopped seeing my therapist on a regular basis and was doing a maintenance routine. Basically I didn't feel I needed constant therapy anymore. Yeah, right! I needed it more than ever. My wife and I started arguing more and more to the point where we couldn't be in the same room with each other without commenting negatively on something. After a couple of weeks, she and the kids convinced me I needed to start up full time again. I still felt I knew myself better than they did. I fought them for a while but eventually gave in and started therapy.

I have been going weekly now ever since and it's the best thing I've ever done. I needed this more than I knew. There are so many things still trapped in my brain that we are working weekly to try and get out. My personality has improved 100%. My confidence abilities are getting better daily and I'm so proud of myself for all my accomplishments. Ten years ago I wouldn't have been able to make that statement.

There have been many changes that have taken place in my life since round two of PTSD. My wife and I are separated, going on two years now. The funny thing about that is we get along so much better now than we ever did. She and my kids are my biggest support system. I wouldn't be where I am today without them all. They were the ones who helped me decide to write this book. I had wanted to write one for years. Someone once said to me that I should write a book and show the world what I've seen. The first thing I thought was why would I want to share the nightmares I've seen. Then along came PTSD and I felt if I could help just one person who's going through what I am, then it's all worth it. So, here it is. Again, not everything I've experienced in my life as a firefighter/EMT is in this book; I need to save something for book #2!

My bottom line is, PTSD is a disease that affects the best people in the worst ways. It's not the end of the world. It's not a death sentence either. It's more of a pain in the ass for anyone who tries their hardest to help those in need. I stand before you, exposed and vulnerable, saying loud and proud, my name is Paul D. Barnes, Sr., I'm a firefighter/EMT and I have PTSD!

A Word From The Family

Paul is such a good man. I'm so proud of all he's been through and how strong he is.

He's easily my best friend simply because he's kind and he's gentle. He patiently answers my daily questions: what's wrong with my Jeep? (How about now?) (Um, and now?) He's incredibly supportive.

PTSD stole that from me for awhile. It took my husband, my best friend and the father of my children—my only children—and left me with a shell. A shell who hurt, who raged, who asked me questions I just couldn't answer.

Then it got worse.

Paul learned to manage his symptoms two years after he was originally diagnosed. For about ten years, there was peace in our home. Laughter, again. Love.

But PTSD returned like the bitch it is.

Paul is holding on—tightly—and he's doing a wonderful job. He's intact, his integrity is intact.

There's nothing I can say about that stupid disease that you haven't heard before. I hate it. I hate watching him hurt; knowing he may need me but that he won't ask for my help.

In the end, it has to be enough that he's here. He's okay. He's doing the best he can and that's all I can ask. I'm so proud of the example he sets as a firefighter, an EMT, an instructor, an evaluator, a daddy, a friend and now an author. I'm grateful that he supports me and our children, even our fluffy pup, as we find where we need to be.

Thank you for supporting him.

Fiona Barnes

07/03/15

My dad is the strongest man I know. He gives his all to his job, every shift, while still being a supportive, devoted father. With PTSD, my dad has shown me what it means to be brave. He hasn't stopped fighting, he hasn't given in to the disease, and I know he never would. He has taught me that during life's worst times, it's okay to ask for help when you can't do it alone. I would do anything for him as he would do anything for me.

Andrew Barnes

My dad is amazing in what he does. Even through the struggles he has been faced with, he brings an amazing face to his job, the very thing that gave him his disease. I feel like PTSD has made him stronger, more patient and more assertive. He is an amazing father, a great support to my mom, a fantastic writer, funny and understanding.

I think of him when I do or hear something cool or need advice. And I know I will always get a great answer.

When life hands him lemons, he makes lemonade and shares it with everyone. He always gives more than he takes. I love my dad very much and I know that all of the wonderful things he has done will come back to him.

Lexi Barnes

About The Author

Born and raised in Connecticut, Paul grew up in a suburban neighborhood. He joined the United States Air Force at the age of eighteen and spent six years as a military police officer. After leaving the service, Paul became a dispatcher for the Connecticut State Police, then a 911 dispatcher, before becoming a career firefighter.

Paul joined the fire service as a volunteer at the age of sixteen. He also became an Emergency Medical Technician. He's held every position possible with the fire service up to assistant deputy chief before becoming paid.

He is thinking about his next book.

"I just want more!"

PTSD is not curable but it is managable with the right therapy and support. Family, friends and coworkers are key figures in keeping those of us with this disease alive and well. Yes, I said alive. Too often, someone with PTSD takes their own life due to the demons running rampant in their mind. Thankfully, my demons are caged and under control. Every once in a while, one of those little bastards escapes and starts causing problems. That's where my family, friends and therapist come in to corral him and lock him away where he belongs. I'll have this for the rest of my life but I'm living proof that it can be managed and it can be overcome.

"..hopeful. Honest.."

"If you've ever wondered about a day in the life of a firefighter/EMT, here you go."

"Many parts made me cry."

Paul is a veteran firefighter/EMT with 37 years experience. He lives near the shore in Connecticut.

When The Laughter Dies:
A True Account of A Firefighter/EMT & His Struggle With PTSD

Paul D. Barnes, Sr.

Made in the USA
Middletown, DE
31 May 2021